Praise for

a D(

As a fan of negotiation theory and a lover of great story-telling, *Once Upon a Deal...* makes the theory really come alive through entertaining and compelling anecdotes. From negotiating with the EU to negotiating with your mother and from negotiating the price of a hotel room to negotiating with your dog to keep him from chasing grouse, this book shows how having a solid negotiation plan will always get you better results. *Once Upon a Deal...* will show you how to think like Stephen Hawking and Abraham Lincoln and even show you how to negotiate a gold medal at the Olympic Games. It takes an academically proven theory, on which Scotwork's world-class training is based, and illuminates it through a wonderful collection of stories. You'll earn the price of the book back a thousand-fold!

Ben Ficke – Global Procurement Director, Whitbread

An outstanding compilation that allows us to draw up the experiences of others to help with your own negotiation journey.

Bobby Singh – SVP, Global Commercial Officer, WPP

As a publisher, I believe in the power of storytelling and *Once Upon a Deal...* applies this most effective tool to the art of negotiation. These stories, distilled from years of knowledge and application, and told in an engaging, absorbing manner will enhance any reader's skills in this area.

David Young – Retired CEO of Hachette Book Group, USA

Once Upon a Deal... distils complex negotiating theory into a series of simple, practical, thought-provoking stories that will not only entertain you but may well save you a couple of quid too.

Ali Cowen – Group Head of People, Beck-Pollitzer

If more business books were as useful, concise and fun to read as *Once Upon a Deal...*, the business world would be a better place. Enlightened with witty anecdotes and valuable lessons on life, work and negotiations... and whether we admit it or not, many of us will relate to the characters and situations in its pages! A go to reference book for anyone involved in the complex world of negotiation.

Steven Mills – Procurement Transformation Director, Thales UK

It's not often that a nonfiction book is exciting, but not only does this book excite, it expands the mind and creates an incredible space to think, learn and shape. Turning naturally dull subjects into intriguing, mind blowing pieces of wisdom. Your brain is taken on an empowering journey, giving you the hunger to learn.

Lucy Mills – HR/L&D Manager, SPAR

An invaluable guide to life – I just wish I'd read it 30 years ago!

Jane Garvey – Award Winning Broadcaster

Once Upon a Deal... not only offers insightful, thought provoking strategies and analysis, it also provides real world practical advice on how to navigate and succeed in the of the art of negotiation. Horace has managed to distil his vast experience into a simple but compelling read. A fantastic for tool for all.

Amadu Sowe – Senior Vice President, Paramount

A lively and entertaining guide to the often undervalued art of negotiation that is full of practical advice and tips on how to end up with the best possible deal.

Jonathan Prynn – Associate Editor, Evening Standard

Once Upon a Deal... is illustrative of everything Scotwork does so well: story-telling at its best combined with immediately useful tips & skills. In fact, it's the second-best book Scotwork have written: number one is the little blue Filofax I got from the course which still refer to daily 6 years on.

John Philliskirk – Senior Manager Consulting, PwC

Once Upon a Deal...

Stories about
life, work & negotiation

edited by Horace McDonald

First published in Great Britain by Practical Inspiration Publishing, 2023

© Horace McDonald, 2023

The moral rights of the author have been asserted

ISBN   9781788604116   (print)
        9781788604130   (epub)
        9781788604123   (mobi)

Every effort has been made to trace copyright holders and to obtain their permission for the use of copyright material. The publisher apologises for any errors or omissions and would be grateful if notified of any corrections that should be incorporated in future reprints or editions of this book.

Want to bulk-buy copies of this book for your team and colleagues? We can customise the content and co-brand *Once Upon a Deal…* to suit your business's needs.

Please email info@practicalinspiration.com for more details.

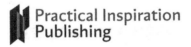

TABLE OF CONTENTS

Preface

Once Upon a Deal... – Stories of life, work & negotiation

Since its inception in 1975, Scotwork's founders, John McMillan and Stephen White, have transformed Scotwork into a global business working with clients to improve their deal outcomes through enhancing capability in commercial negotiation. We have taught more people, in more languages, in more countries than any of our competitors. By an odd quirk of fate, as I write this, we've recently been asked to run a course in Iceland, which would be a first for Scotwork.

Our aim is to 'transform the way the world negotiates' with a teaching model designed to encourage participants to strive to develop outcomes that enhance value for both parties. To achieve this requires a focus on preparation with clear objectives, developing alternative strategies, understanding the negotiation from both parties' perspectives, testing assumptions through good questioning and listening, and using the information gathered to make a proposal we think the other party can accept. These themes are explored throughout this book. Negotiation is everywhere and despite creating the market for negotiation training and the emergence of a number of worthy rivals, it is still a subject that is largely under-taught in business schools and under-funded in the workplace. We strive to ensure that we grow our business through delighting our existing clients across the world and engaging new customers, helping them all to transform businesses through effective negotiation to drive better deals.

We have taken a different approach to adding to the canon of knowledge in negotiation. It is not our purpose to use this book to 'teach' its readers how to negotiate more effectively, which is a common approach. We strongly believe that negotiation is a learned skill and, in the same way that you can't learn to fly a plane from reading a book, negotiation capability is enhanced through practice and experience in work and life, making mistakes and getting advice from people with more knowledge, *and* by attending a training course.

This book is founded in an understanding that humans comprehend the world through stories and commonly held myths. These are vital to the functioning of modern societies as the concept of money, the functioning of the state, governance and hierarchies only exist through humans being able to retain and adhere to a set of commonly held beliefs. The stories in this book were originally published as weekly online blogs, with the aim of telling a compelling story while providing the reader with some insight into a particular area of negotiation. These stories are often topical, sometimes personal, but always aim to expand the reader's knowledge of negotiation. They have been selected from over 350 stories written and published through our social media channels since our last book *The Real Deal* in 2014.

In the period since publishing our last book, the UK has been through Brexit and the world through a global pandemic. Many of the stories written were based on these events and a number of these have been included. Some of the stories will have been superseded by subsequent events.

On occasion, we ask you to slip into a virtual time machine: the stories often depict a moment in time but the negotiation principles are timeless. This book has not been designed to be read cover to cover, let alone chapter by chapter, but has been constructed as a reference book. If you'd like to gain some insight or refresh knowledge in a particular area of negotiation, reading a few of the stories in a chapter will help, regardless of the type of negotiation you're involved in. Whether you're reading this with no knowledge of Scotwork and negotiation, are an ex-participant, or have been given the book at the end of a Scotwork course, we'd like you to enjoy it by dipping in and out to refresh or enhance your knowledge in bite-sized chunks.

Happy dipping…

Horace McDonald
CEO – Scotwork UK

Introduction

Once Upon a Deal...

Negotiation is everywhere. It is played out amongst parents and children, by friends with friends, between colleagues in the workplace and externally with clients and suppliers. When countries are at loggerheads, economic systems are in peril and at times of political instability you'll rarely listen to a news bulletin without hearing the word 'negotiation'. Irrespective of the job you do, or where you are in the world, you will encounter it daily. Scotwork believes it is a learned skill, best taught in a classroom, and our objective in this book is to bring some of our core principles to life through storytelling.

While negotiation is all around us, we would not advocate that one should approach every negotiation situation with the same rigour as outlined in this book. If you impose a condition on your partner every time they ask you for something, you're likely to bring the relationship to a juddering halt. At Scotwork, our proposition is focused on developing capability in the commercial sphere; however, the core principles apply to every negotiation. On a personal level, how many times have you come away from even the simplest of negotiation situations and reflected on how differently you would have approached it if you'd applied some core principles?

Before I start to provide you with more details on how this book works, it's important to first understand why negotiation is relevant and, just as importantly, where it is not. Negotiation is one of a number of options that can be employed to resolve conflict. It is important to recognise that it is not appropriate in all circumstances. For example, at one extreme, if you have the power to bend the other party to your will and impose your solution on them, then that is the most appropriate option and you should use it, as it won't cost you anything. Likewise, at the other extreme, if you have nothing to offer either by way of something they want or something you cannot take away that they need, then you have no option but to concede to their demands and are not in a position to negotiate.

In the commercial world, negotiation is a given as both parties have power due to them either having something the other party wants (which we term **incentives**) or being in a position to impose an undesirable condition or withdraw a benefit to the other party (which we term a **sanction**). It is important to understand that negotiation comes at a cost. Even as negotiation experts, we would rather not negotiate if we could avoid it, as it always going to cost something. When, as is often the case, negotiation is the best option to resolve a conflict, the key is to ensure that the benefits accrued from the negotiation outweigh the costs, whether they be tangible or intangible, as this is how value is created.

The 8-Steps of the Scotwork negotiation framework were developed from watching thousands of hours of union negotiations dating back to 50 years ago. Irrespective of the negotiation scenario you find yourself in, at any point on the negotiation journey you will be using one of the 8-Steps. Think of the framework as a map: regardless of where you are on the journey, the map will signpost where you are and where to move to next, thus giving you control of the negotiation process.

The 8-Step Scotwork Framework

Prepare	Advanced preparation as standard
Argue	Conducting constructive negotiating dialogue
Signal	Spotting / rewarding / encouraging flexibility
Propose	How to make and receive
Package	Reshaping to close the gap
Bargain	Trading to close the gap
Close	When and how to close
Agree	From agreement to effective implementation

There are two things about the framework that are important to note:

- It is not linear; while Step 1 is **Preparation** and Step 8 is **Agree**, most negotiations don't move seamlessly through Steps 1 to 8. For example, a negotiation may start with you receiving a **Proposal** (Step 4) from which you might consider it appropriate to go back to **Preparation** (Step 1) or **Argue** (Step 2).
- Not all negotiations require you to use each of the eight steps. However, knowledge of them is important as this will help guide you through the negotiation process.

Negotiations come in all shapes and sizes: some are very simple (in the commercial world price and volume usually feature) and some are hugely complex where they can consist of dozens of variables, each with a different value to both sides, can take months or years to complete and can serve to underpin a business or political relationship for decades.

The stories in this book are designed to provide relevance and context to each step in the framework, give the reader a deeper understanding of each step and bring the steps to life for the reader through aligning each of the steps with a real-life situation.

The 8-Step framework forms the basis of the chapters in this book, and we have taken a linear approach running through Steps 1 to 8. Due to the nature of how negotiation plays out, particularly in the public eye, certain chapters feature more stories than others and many of the stories cover more than one of the steps.

The stories range from the serious to the light-hearted and they are meant to be informative and enjoyable. For example, in 'Six-second delay' from the **Argue** Chapter, Alan Smith tells a story about the importance of managing one's emotional state and contrasts Donald Trump, as the ultimate 'chimp' whose 'reptilian brain' responds to everything around him, with Ed Milliband, who adopts a strategy of giving himself six seconds before responding to any questions posed to him in live interviews as a way of delivering more considered answers. By contrast, Romana Henry, one of our resident sports fanatics, tells a story about 'When persuasion doesn't work' in the **Propose** Chapter based on her advice to a regular running partner whose brother was being made redundant. With some creative thinking, she came up with an imaginative counterproposal to resolve a difficult issue that enabled him to exit the business on more favourable terms.

In the **Prepare** Chapter, Stephen White's 'My mother and the EU' rails against politicians and business leaders who predict certainty in the future and build deterministic strategies based on these positions. Good negotiators (including Stephen's mother) understand that the future is uncertain and preparing different strategies to accommodate a multitude of possible outcomes is a smart approach.

Thank yous

I would like to take this opportunity to thank the Scotwork blog group past and present who have contributed stories over the last eight years. A particular thanks goes to Stephen White and Alan Smith, who wrote most of the stories in this period and are appropriately represented here. They were ably supported at the time by David Bannister and Robin Copland, and a mention also goes out to Romana Henry, Annabel Shorter, Tom Feinson, Ellis Croft, Ann McAleavy and, of course, our founder, John McMillan. I would also like to acknowledge the people who helped us with this project, Alison Jones from Practical Inspiration Publishing who came up with the title, Mary McCormick from Newgen and Lesley (Wee Bear) Cooper.

A final thank you goes out to Laura (who wanted us to use only her first name), a recent participant on a Scotwork course who sent her tutor Ann Allfrey a most brilliant story of how she used our 8-Step framework to negotiate with her dog to get her out for a walk. At the time of writing the story, Laura was unaware that we were intending to publish a book and I was delighted when she gave us her consent to include it. It's a great way to pull everything we do together and is such a wonderful story in its own right; it sits on its own as an epilogue.

Horace McDonald
CEO – Scotwork UK

THE 8-STEPS

CHAPTER 1

EFFECTIVE PREPARATION

Preparation is vital in negotiation; many would argue that it's the most important of the 8-Steps. The more complex the negotiation, the greater the need for preparation; however, this process needs to be gone through for even the most basic negotiations. To maximise its effectiveness, herewith is a checklist of the key components.

- What are my **objectives**? What do I want or need to achieve?
- What are my **must-haves**? The things you must get to do a deal – this requires rigour.
- What are my **intends**? What are the things that I realistically would like to have?
- What is my **strategy** (often confused with objectives)? How will I get there? Also, you need to consider alternative strategies.

- What is my **wish list**? What else can I ask for? Develop this list, ignoring any constraints.
- What is my **concession list**? What can I offer the other party to get my **wish list** items?

Give yourself sufficient time to go through this process; it will serve you well. It is also important to repeat the exercise, looking at the negotiation from the other party's perspective, essentially to walk in their shoes.

If you're working in a team, take the time beforehand to run this process together. It will *always* be time very well spent. You put yourself at a major disadvantage if you go into a negotiation unprepared, particularly if the other party has prepared, which should always be your going-in assumption, not to mention the advantage you get if the converse is true!

In the bubble – How preparation gives you a shot at the title...

Alan Smith

(Published 13th July 2017)

For two weeks of the year, I become a bit of a tennis fan. These weeks coincide with the Wimbledon fortnight, possibly one of the most eagerly awaited tennis tournaments in the world.

When I was much younger, it was the time of year that my friends and I rushed off to the local tennis courts that were usually empty, but now thronged with queues of similarly inspired youths fancying a hit. I thought I was pretty good until I actually played someone who played regularly, and then realised I was pretty useless. Lacked the skills to be honest, but probably didn't have the mindset either. McEnroe-esque in my attitude and verbiage.

Some years ago, Johanna Konta reached the semi-finals of the Wimbledon event, which represented a fantastic display of skill, grit, determination and effort.

Johanna Konta said that she was 'tremendously proud of being part of a little bit of history' after becoming Britain's first women's Wimbledon semi-finalist for 39 years. 'Ever since I was nine years old, I've believed in my own ability and dreamed big,' Konta told BBC Sport. 'I don't give myself too much time to dream and focus on the work.'

What really interests me about professional sports people is their ability to control the situations that they find themselves in and channel their abilities in times of huge stress. Watching Konta at Wimbledon, or Owen Farrell kicking the penalty to tie the series between the British Lions and the All Blacks at Eden Park, they seem to be able to rise above the moment and find the zone. Or, as Tracy Austin described it, 'being in the bubble'.

Being in the bubble requires us to be in control of our own behaviour. The chief thing we need to be able to do in dealing with a difficult or challenging situation, or person, is to control ourselves. That requires preparation. There is a direct relationship between preparation and anxiety: the more prepared you are, the fewer situations you have to deal with on the fly.

Many negotiators turn up to the challenging negotiations they face with little structured planning or forethought. The equivalent to rocking up at Wimbledon in Dunlop Green Flash and expecting to be able to handle the Centre Court.

They simply can't. Or should I say shouldn't.

Fundamental to preparation is to imagine what do I do if things do not go to plan? How do I flex? How do I get out of the way of myself? How can I create time if I need it?

Get that right and you will have a much better shot at the title.

On the ropes – If data is at play, make sure you've mastered it...

Stephen White

(Published 18th May 2017)

For as long as politicians are poorly briefed and manifesto promises incorrectly costed with policies not properly thought through, they will struggle in the face of good interviewers, whose goal is to catch them out on data issues and produce cringe-making sound bites for the entertainment of the public. Laura Kuenssberg's seven-time question to Jeremy Corbyn about his commitment to take the UK out of the EU whatever the deal achieved at the end of the two years (the data-answer to which was a simple 'yes' or 'no') left Corbyn looking unsure of his own policy and was the segment of the interview that led the news, at the expense of a focus on Labour Party policy announcements.

The syndrome is common not just in political interviewing but also in commercial negotiating. Data has become an increasingly important element of the negotiating process; many negotiations don't move forward until conflicts in data and its interpretation are resolved and often these data conflicts become negotiations in themselves. Most salespeople can tell stories of being unprepared for an onslaught of data requests from a buyer for which they had no answers, sometimes because they were ill prepared, or because no one had thought to collect the data in the first place. In the face of these demands the inexperienced mumble and fumble, mis-speak, get confused, lose confidence and end up looking, sounding and feeling stupid, which from the buying side of the table is exactly the objective because a despondent seller does poorer deals.

Of course, the preventative to this embarrassment is good preparation particularly in terms of exploring the negotiating counterparties' likely behaviour, which in this case will include an analysis of the data they might demand, rehearsing the responses which will be most effective and thinking about the unintended consequences that might result. If the then Labour Shadow Home Secretary had revealed that the true cost of adding 10,000 extra police was £300 million not £300,000, the obvious question would become 'where will that money come from?'

But I would argue that the attacking behaviour of the questioner/interviewer is actually often counterproductive. It might make good TV, or shift the power balance in a negotiation, but it is not revelatory of the facts and in a commercial environment will possibly close down any previous plan to engage collaboratively. The spat between Theresa May and the EU bureaucrats about what was said at a dinner at Downing Street is a case in point. Lack of data (the facts) simply sours the relationship and makes future negotiations that bit more difficult. Yes, of course we all know this is just posturing by both sides, but it has pernicious side effects and is better avoided unless there is a specific thought-through objective.

Leverage – Be careful not to underestimate the power you have...

Robin Copland

(Published 22nd March 2018)

So, there I was in the hotel lobby telling the team behind the desk all my woes. This was about the fourth hotel I had been to; no, I didn't have a booking but I had my wife and three children outside in the car and I was kind of desperate; no, I didn't know that there was a major conference in the town that we were visiting, and yes, had I known about it, then I would probably have either avoided the place altogether or, at the very least, booked a family room.

'Oh, you have a family room,' I repeated. Wonderful. A late cancellation? Lucky for us. 'What are the chances of a special deal, given how late in the day it is?' I asked. They just looked at me. It was the kind of look that ET might have expected. It was the kind of look that asked the question, 'What planet are you from?' From a negotiating perspective, it was about all I deserved.

In his book, *The Art of the Deal*, Donald Trump talks about 'leverage'.[1] He writes, 'the worst thing you can possibly do in a deal is seem desperate to make it. That makes the other guy smell blood, and then you're dead. The best thing you can do is

---

[1] D. Trump *The Art of the Deal* (1987)

deal from strength and leverage is the biggest strength you can have. Leverage is having something the other guy wants. Or, better yet, needs.' Colourfully put perhaps, but he has a point. I had made the fatal mistake of not only telling them what I wanted (a good thing, typically), but how badly I needed it. The words 'desperate' and 'good deal' rarely go together.

Victims tend to think that power in a negotiation is a function of size, but we in Scotwork teach that 'power' is derived from that combination of things that the other side wants – or wants to avoid. So, negotiators should, as part of their preparation, have a long, cold look at the power balance. Analyse the other side's needs. Can you address them? Do you have anything in your arsenal that they would rather avoid? Do you have leverage? Then think about it from your perspective. What do they have that you want, or want to avoid?

I am constantly surprised by this answer to the question, 'Who is more powerful in a negotiation, you or the other side?' Just about everyone – whether they be a buyer, seller, manager, employee, or even family member! – says 'the other side'. It is rare that the power balance is one-sided; negotiators often have more power than they think.

But just to add to that, consider this quote from Cheverton and van der Velde in their book *Understanding the Professional Buyer*: 'If you think that the buyer has all the power, then you are probably right.'[2] You can substitute the words 'the other

[2] P. Cheverton and J.P. van der Velde *Understanding the Professional Buyer: What Every Sales Professional Should Know About How the Modern Buyer Thinks and Behaves* (2010)

side' for 'buyer'. Here is the nub of the problem for a victim. They convince themselves that the other side has all the power and, in so doing, they actually concede the power balance to their opponents! How often do negotiators strike bad deals because they don't analyse the power balance more effectively?

My advice is clear: don't be a victim; don't underestimate your power in a negotiation; spend time in preparation and during the negotiation, analysing and thinking about the power balance and, instead of ceding the power to the other side in your head, or by your actions, analyse the situation forensically. To use Trump's word again, give yourself some leverage.

The infinite negotiation monkey cage
– Preparation and practice makes perfect...

Alan Smith

(Published 29th September 2016)

I can state with pretty near certainty, and I admit comfort, that my dentist knows something about teeth. Partly because the last time I went to see him with a damaged filling I left with it fixed, which frankly would have been difficult for someone without any knowledge of teeth to have achieved. Unless of course he had been very lucky that day and managed to wing it.

He also has a diploma on the wall, which suggests that he gave a good account of himself in his exams and had to look at a few thousand other teeth before he asked to look at mine, with a modicum of success.

This got me thinking about a piano recital my wife and I went to recently. Not something I'd ever done before, and to be honest, something I suspect I will never do again. It was at a theatre near where we live. I can't say the pianist's name with any degree of skill either (so she must be good).

I reasonably expected her to get some pretty good sounds to emit from the piano. It would be rare indeed to have a pianist who was coming to the end of what appears to have been a long tour, to have sold out purely by a random act of erratically pounding the ivories of a baby grand.

But how many of us can claim the same level of certainty about the skill level of either ourselves or our counterpart when we enter the negotiation room to conduct a business discussion around a commercially sensitive contract, complaint or conflict?

Now I know there is possibly no such thing as the perfect deal, where both parties achieve the absolute best deal by trading and creating value in the optimum way and have the appropriate skill level to engage the other side to do the same in a largely consensual way.

But I also know that for many of us the negotiation is a largely unplanned and unrehearsed affair. In the classrooms we teach in, and scarily the boardrooms we consult in, the strategy we are most often told they will adopt is the one where they will 'wait and see what the other side does', and then act.

My worry is that the most I can infer is that the people on either side of the table (or all the sides in a multilateral discussion) have a track record. The direction of that track may not be particularly good, but it does exist.

Of course, some people are instinctively better than others. But even instincts need to be refined and honed. Maybe in the classroom, or perhaps by a good coach, one on one.

Even natural born winners can be improved, like the dentist and pianist, by practice. Leave chance to the infinite negotiation monkey cage. It might even work eventually.

My mother and the EU – Beware of making the future a certainty...

Stephen White

(Published 25th February 2016)

We have a problem with my mother. She is a gregarious 90-year-old, has successfully lived on her own since my Dad died 10 years ago, is full of life and bright as a button, has lots of friends, and goes out to play cards five times a week. Until three weeks ago when her arthritic knees gave up, and she became virtually immobile. She can hobble around her small apartment with the aid of a three-wheeled 'walker', but the stairs are impossible, and she lives one floor up in a building without an elevator. She has become housebound.

So, she and the family have some decisions to make. Do we try to find a ground floor flat, which would allow her to go out, at least as far as a taxi that could take her to her friends and the shops? Should we aim for a warden-assisted flat, where there would be a speedy rescue service if she fell over? Or should we find a residential care home where she could make new friends and spend the rest of her life (and we hope it will be a long one) being looked after?

The answer, to a large part, depends on whether we take a shorter or longer view. Installing her in a more accessible flat works as long as she has some mobility, but if that mobility goes altogether, we will then have to move her again to a care home. Or maybe we would then employ a carer who would come to live in, in which case we need now to choose the new flat with living accommodation for the carer if we want to avoid the upheaval of her having to move again.

Last week I asked her what her preference was. 'I don't know,' she said. 'I have no experience of this situation and I don't know what is going to happen in the future, so how can I know what the best decision will be?'

When David Cameron brought back a deal from his summit with the leaders of the 27 other EU members, he felt he could recommend to voters that Britain should stay in the EU on the basis of this deal. As predicted, a number of his cabinet colleagues, and many others, came out publicly with the opposite recommendation. The electorate will vote 'in' or 'out' in a referendum on 23rd June, and until then both sides will batter us with facts and figures about the dangers of taking the opposite position to their own.

They need to start thinking like my mother.

A classic example of woolly thinking about the EU came from Theo Paphitis, a well-known UK businessman talking on the *Question Time* programme on BBC TV. Answering a question about whether David Cameron has done enough to persuade the public to vote to stay in the EU, he said, 'At the moment I just have not got a [clue] which side to go on. When will we be told the facts? Not scaremongering that the earth is flat and that if we leave the EU we will fall off the

edge, or that Brexit is the best thing since sliced bread....
There have been no facts.'

Sorry to disappoint you, Theo, but there are no facts
because this decision is about a future event, and unless you
are a registered clairvoyant the best you can do is form an
opinion based on a mixture of historical facts (of which there
are too many to assimilate, not too few) and hypothesis.
What might be best for Britain and for the EU depends on so
many unknowns. What if the UK economy collapses? What if
Russia invades Ukraine proper? What if the Eurozone disin-
tegrates? What if Donald Trump is the next US President?

So, those politicians who are categorical about what will
happen in terms of sovereignty, our ability to renegotiate, the
legal status of the deal before treaty changes and so on, and if
we stay in the EU or vote to leave, are talking through their
bottom halves. Like my mother, they have no experience of
a scenario like this, nor which one of their hypotheses will
actually play out. Scotwork's experience of watching thousands of negotiations every year is that however many 'what
ifs' you plan for, what actually happens is likely to be something you didn't see coming! That doesn't mean that planning
is a waste of time, but it does mean that retaining flexibility of
approach is all-important.

And one more comparison with my mother's situation.
She knows that the decision she has to make is affected by
the time frame. The best decision for the next two years,
while she still has some mobility, might become a poor
decision if she then has to go through a second upheaval
because she subsequently cannot continue to live on her
own. Similarly, what is best for Britain has to be measured

against a timeline – are we talking the best for the next five years, 15 years or 50 years?

Politicians on both sides need to wise up and take advice from my mother. She has the humility to know that she doesn't know the right answer for everything but that she does know how to go about thinking things through. She won't pay any special heed to family members who take dogmatic positions. Instead, she will carefully evaluate the opinions she hears and then quietly make her own mind up.

We should not be surprised. In the words of comedian Peter Kay, 'If it's not one thing, it's your mother.'

The computer says 'no'... – Computers manage tasks, negotiation requires skill...

Horace McDonald

(Published 21st October 2021)

A frequent tennis partner of mine asked my opinion on an article in *The Guardian* suggesting that artificial intelligence (AI) and mathematics will play a bigger role in international diplomacy in the future. Despite being a life-long *Guardian* reader, I'd missed the article as most of my consumption is now at the weekend, while sitting in bed with a cup of coffee (one of the great benefits of no longer having to run around after young children).

The idea was postulated by Michael Ambühl, a Professor of Negotiation and Conflict Management and a former chief Swiss-EU negotiator. He claims that while the use of data science, AI and machine learning are in their infancy, machine learning has been used to assess the integrity of data and detect fake news to ensure the diplomatic process has reliable foundations. In the article, Ambühl states that, as Switzerland's chief EU negotiator, he ran game theory simulations ahead of talks that led to Switzerland joining the Schengen (EU Border-Free Travel Area) and a raft of agreements with the EU on tax, trade and security.[3] The analysis indicated that it was in Switzerland's interest for the negotiations to take place as a package rather than sequentially, and so the Swiss government insisted on this as a basis for talks.

That they would think about running the negotiation sequentially is interesting. As experts in negotiation, we would always advise keeping as many areas open as possible, as it allows for more creativity and enhanced value creation. Bearing this in mind, running the negotiation as a total package allows, for example, the Swiss to take value in areas of high importance, say, trade, in return for making concessions in, say, tax. I'll leave you to make up your own mind on the Swiss attitudes to the latter, it's just an example. The more variables brought to the table and traded in a negotiation, the greater the opportunity to create value.

Based on this, negotiation, like most things in business, is simple. Here at Scotwork we place a significant focus on preparation. In short, expert negotiators understand their **must-haves** and their **intends**, i.e. where they can be flexible. In this phase, consideration is also given to a range of strategies that can be adopted to achieve one's objectives. A key skill is to create an environment that encourages the other party to

---

[3] www.theguardian.com/world/switzerland

work similarly, and at Scotwork we manage this in the **Argue** and **Signal** Steps. This enables both parties to outline how they see the negotiation and the extent to which it accords with the other party's views. Any discrepancies in understanding and approach are managed here and, by establishing a sound basis for co-operation, a framework is built to provide a positive outlook for both parties. However, what often makes matters more difficult is people. Our competitive nature often acts to inhibit sharing of information, wanting to force our will on the other party and asking for too much in return for what we want to give. This creates a climate of mistrust, and whereas a collaborative outlook from both parties can work to build value, a competitive mindset destroys it.

My response to my tennis partner was that it will be some time before machine learning plays a significant part at the table in commercial negotiations, where the bulk of the information at play is not in the public domain, and for each party their approach to the negotiation is likely to be heavily focused on situational factors. What is undeniable is that data analysis will play a huge part in helping companies understand and derive commercial advantage to take to the negotiating table. My son works as a Business Intelligence Officer building complex models to help clients understand the effectiveness of their digital campaigns and tells me that Google have forecast that every company will have a data department within the next five years. I certainly agree that data and its manipulation will play a significant role in the future. However, human interaction will dominate how negotiations are managed and run for a very long time...

Another fine mess! – The perils of poor teamwork...

Alan Smith

(Published 17th January 2019)

Ever found yourself in that nightmare scenario when you are in front of another party in a negotiation and the partner you have taken to the meeting with you seems to have gone off track, starts revealing new information, conceding on issues that you had both agreed before the negotiation, being conciliatory when they should have been tough or tough when they should have been conciliatory?

Even worse, the other side have picked up on this and have started to focus on your colleague, even though you had agreed to lead the negotiation?

A lot of this can be solved by being thoroughly prepared for the negotiation and having a clear plan, but it can be tough in the real world when your partner (who may even be your boss!) starts to go rogue.

If you have seen the fantastic movie *Stan and Ollie*, you can see just how easy it can be to go off track, and how in the case of Laurel and Hardy it can set the tone for the rest of your life.[4]

Stan Laurel and Oliver Hardy were at the height of their powers in the 1930s, making successful films for the legendary producer Hal Roach. Roach was born in 1892 in New York. After a tough life working as a mule skinner, wrangler and gold prospector, among other things, he wound

---

[4] Sony Pictures *Stan and Ollie* (2018)

up in Hollywood and began picking up jobs as an extra in comedies. By all accounts, including his own, he was a terrible actor, but he saw a future in the movie business and in producing movies, particularly comedies.

His relationship as the producer for Laurel and Hardy was very much on his terms. He paid the two stars (superstars as they would be today) a salary, which meant that despite their success, they remained relatively poor, taking no share of the box office, which frankly is how most successful actors make the big money: this set up was pretty rare in those days. Ever noticed how many A-List actors have 'Executive Producer' credits?

The other clever move was to keep Laurel and Hardy on separate and unsynchronised contracts. When Laurel's contract came up for renewal they both agreed to ask for changes, which Roach refused. Hardy then did not stick to their plan and carried on making films for Roche without Laurel, which resulted in the pair falling out of favour with the public and caused both to lose out.

On screen Hardy was the father figure to the more innocent Laurel but off-screen their personalities were very different, with Laurel being the more serious professional. While Hardy was happy leaving his work behind when he left the set to go gambling or play golf, Laurel was a workaholic, refining scripts and film takes long into the night.

These differences did not help them as a team, and Roach seemed to be able to pull them apart despite their obvious respect, admiration and indeed love for each other.

What's the answer to these challenges? Well, if you find yourself unable to control your colleague despite all the preparation and practice you can afford, and that taking time out during the meeting to get it back on track still doesn't work, then my advice is to not take them with you. Take someone else or just do it yourself with their authority.

For Hardy maybe he would have been able to maintain the partnership with Laurel more profitably by breaking it for the negotiation. It certainly got them into a fine mess by not doing it together.

Another red line breached – Inflexibility is a straitjacket in negotiation...

Robin Copland

(Published 30ᵗʰ May 2019)

When the then Prime Minister, Theresa May, resigned, having failed to get her Brexit deal through Parliament, it was the first time in living memory that a British Prime Minister had resigned because of a failure to negotiate an appropriate deal. Whether a deal to suit all colours of opinion was ever available is another matter altogether. However, May talked of the need to compromise in her resignation speech in Downing Street and, to be fair, had she the benefit of Doctor Who's Tardis when she came to power in 2016, she might well have listened carefully to those words in her future before she set out all her 'red lines', called an unnecessary general election and refused steadfastly to involve just about anyone outside her own inner circle as she negotiated her ill-fated deal with the EU; the deal that for the EU became non-negotiable.

Here's the thing. Strip away all the personalities, forget the negotiating process itself, look at the deal in the cold light of a 52:48 referendum result and it suddenly begins to look as if it has the makings of a workable solution to the problem. Maintenance of close economic links but without the twin straitjackets of the common agricultural and fisheries policies, nor indeed the dead hand of Brussels' bureaucracy.

But then there is Ireland – some might say that the backstop was the nail in the coffin, but the truth of the matter is that Ireland had featured little in the Brexit debate previously. It was a non-issue – not even discussed except, obviously, in Northern Ireland itself. Neither side in the debate seemed to spend much time thinking about the close north-south links that had been developed as part of the Good Friday agreement and that had done so much to begin the healing process between all but the most ardent and extreme on both sides of the divide. How to square a circle?

And the ultimate irony in all of this was May's ill-timed general election that removed her majority in the House of Commons and threw her to the wolves of the Democratic Unionist Party, a group of MPs who do not even reflect the majority of opinion in Northern Ireland.

So, a failure to apply basic negotiating skills and it has come to this. How can the new Prime Minister move things forward?

- Early engagement in private talks before any public promises are made would be a start. And to your left, flying through the sky over there? That's a flock of flying pigs. Careful now. It's got you. Best get that cleaned;
- Early engagement with all sides of the House of Commons. You may need some votes from across the house;

- Clear guiding principles, that lead to...
- A clear set of realistic objectives;
- As few 'red lines' as is possible;
- A credible threat – Boris Johnson, love him or hate him, had at least come out and not ruled 'no deal' off the table;
- The flexibility to realise that to achieve some important goals, some less important goals may need to be traded off the table;
- As little 'blind faith' as possible and certainly to keep any 'triumphalism' down to a muted whisper;
- In terms of negotiating tactics, a lot of 'just suppose' and 'what ifs' might be a useful start.

Interesting times!

Negotiating advice for politicians –
When will they ever learn...

Stephen White

(Published 7th May 2015)

On the day this story is published, the population of the UK votes in elections for their next government. Opinion polls put the two main parties neck and neck, with neither commanding a strong enough following to win an outright majority. So, the result is likely to be a minority government which will have to form a coalition or make deals with the handful of minor parties in order to be able to govern. Even if there is an outright majority for one party, the margin will be so small that alliances would need to be forged for effective government to survive. In the UK's first-past-the-post system, this is rare.

Do we have a cadre of politicians who can rise to the challenge of creating these deals through effective and inspired negotiating? Based on the debacle when they tried to do the same thing in 2010 the answer is likely to be 'no'. Most self-confessed negotiating experts in business talk a better game than they play, and politicians are no different. Look at the sparkling performances in negotiations between the EU and Greece, between the P5+1 and Iran, between the Quartet, Israel and the Palestinians, between Indonesia and Australia (for those readers who don't recognise irony, this is irony). The list is shamefully long.

So, with suitable humility and an expectation that it will all be ignored, I offer some advice to the politicians who find themselves over the next few weeks trying to do what we mere mortals do every day of our working lives – turning situational problems into workable solutions using simple and effective negotiating techniques.

1. **Wait a few days before you start**. If you are already meeting other parties within 48 hours of the end of polling, you are being premature. Let the dust settle, the final result be known and analysed, and give yourself some time for negotiation preparation. The country will not descend into anarchy for the want of a weekend, nor will global bankers drive the currency into oblivion during that time;

2. **Get over yourselves**. The people have spoken, and if nothing else their common message is that they do not

like nor trust any of you. If you approach the negotiations with an objective of getting your own way on behalf of the 30% or so who voted for you, then you have failed to see the bigger picture. Voters are telling you to stop being prima donnas and start being effective managers of the country, dogma or no dogma;

3. **Enough with the red lines and tablets of stone already**. All they do is box you into a negotiating corner, which isn't helpful at all. Voters have as much belief in their long-term validity as they have in you, which based on the result of the election is not very much. We all know there will have to be negotiated compromise; what you need to be able to do is look for nuances in the way that issues which are important to you are treated so that you can allow them to be included in the negotiated settlement. And if your counterparty continues to bang on about a policy you simply can't live with, insist that either they change their team, or you change your prospective partners;

4. **Don't grandstand**. The public want to be kept informed of progress, not dazzled by bombast or harangued by derogatory comments about everyone else. The real constituency who needs to be convinced consists of your fellow Members of the House of Commons – elected by the millions to represent them in just this type of situation. So save your consultations and explanations for them and involve them regularly;

5. **Don't believe the rumours**. In 2010, one of the two main parties was suckered into making concessions to the Lib Dems on proportional voting because they believed rumours that the other main party had already offered it.

Negotiators sometimes mis-speak, politicians frequently mis-speak, so I expect that negotiating politicians do little else but mis-speak; and

6. **Be constructive.** An indecisive election result does not mean that the electorate are dithering wastrels. It means they don't like all of any of the manifestos, or that they are so divided in their views that any mandate you think you have to impose your manifesto will not represent a sensible form of democracy. This means that you have to construct something new out of the ashes – a set of implementable ideas that have broad appeal, a realistic degree of achievability, and the creativity which comes from an analysis of the problems to be dealt with, not the power which is wielded.

Who prepares wins! – If you fail to plan, you plan to fail – Abraham Lincoln

Alan Smith

(Published 10th January 2019)

I am a big fan of the Channel 4 programme called *Who Dares Wins.*

In it, civilians are invited to take part in the rigorous selection process used by the British elite special operations division, the SAS. The programme has ex-special forces members barking viciously at the individuals who have elected to take part, and they constantly harangue the participants as they take part in arduous physical and mental challenges while asking if they have had enough and want to hand in their arm band, which signals dismissal from the show.

It has made TV stars of Ant Middleton and Jason (Foxy) Fox, who frankly you wouldn't want to meet on a dark night (unless they were on your side).

One of the things that always surprises me about these sort of reality shows is the fact that some of the participants seem surprised about what they are being asked to do! Now don't get me wrong, if this was a new show, they would have an excuse, but it isn't. There have been a number of seasons. A bit like when the contestants on *I'm a Celebrity* claim to be scared of creepy crawlers. Where have they been?

These participants are soon weeded out, or not in the case of *I'm a Celebrity*, as the general public seem intent on keeping the really scared in and making them suffer.

Preparation, as anyone knows, is probably the most important thing we can do, be that for a TV show, an exam, a marathon or indeed a commercial negotiation.

If you want to be in a strong negotiating position, taking time to prepare is absolutely critical. If you have not done your homework chances are that the other party may very well gain the upper hand in the negotiation, particularly if they have done theirs!

I do appreciate that the world we inhabit moves at an alarming pace, and we are surrounded by pressures and commitments. More is better, but some is better than none at all.

During negotiation preparation, you should spend time on your objectives (and theirs), think about power, think about variables and value creation. In short, spend time figuring out what you want and how you are going to get it.

Abraham Lincoln is one of the many who have been credited with the phrase, 'If you fail to plan, you plan to fail'. Being thoroughly prepared may not guarantee a win, but it will certainly help.

Cinq à sept – A creative use of time (one of the most important variables in negotiation)...

Stephen White

(Published 14ᵗʰ January 2016)

One of the defining qualities of a good negotiator is the ability to manufacture unusual tradeable variables apparently out of thin air. An example of this is how time is used as a variable. Most people would agree that a day comprises 24 hours. But management consultants know that a day in terms of charging fees is more likely to be seven hours, so clients who need more than seven hours find themselves paying for more than a day. Car rental companies define a day as any period up to 24 hours, so clients who want less than that still have to pay for the full 24 hours. So a 'usual' day becomes subverted into an 'unusual' day with a little creative thinking.

Most hotels define a day, or to be more accurate a night, as 19 or 20 hours (check in at 3.00pm, vacate the room by 10.00am or 11.00am). A website, Dayuse.com, enables hotels to take advantage of the opportunity of renting rooms for a shorter period during the day, when they are mainly unoccupied anyway.

International travellers may have experienced this concept already. A number of on-airport hotels operate a similar scheme for the convenience of transit passengers who fly into an airport in the morning but don't depart on their next flight until much later the same day. But Dayuse.com are opening up the opportunity to city centre hotels to earn revenue in the same way.

So, who would use a hotel bedroom only during the day? I don't think you need to ask! The French have long been aware of this opportunity for a couple of hours in the afternoon. Indeed, one expression they use for having an affair is 'cinq à sept' because in the time window from 5.00pm to 7.00pm it is easy to disappear.[5] Whatever you are actually doing, you could be shopping, or stuck on the Périphérique or the Metro, or picking up the kids, or in any number of places which put you out of sight for a couple of hours with a perfectly plausible excuse if you need one.

Dayuse.com say that only 20% of their bookings are from airport transit passengers; the rest are 'business' or 'leisure' users. The price of a day-use hotel room is typically half of the nightly rate or even less, which makes expensive five-star hotels affordable for users, and gives the hotels additional income, not only for the room but for the room service (champagne, roses) which might also be ordered – everyone wins.

So, next time you struggle for a way to use a time variable creatively think of cinq à sept.

---

[5] Cinq à sept is a French-language term for activities taking place after work and before returning home (overtime can be used as an excuse sometimes). It can also mean having dinner (roughly between 5.00 pm and 7.00 pm).

THE 8-STEPS

CHAPTER 2

THE ARGUE STEP

This step is about information sharing and curiosity. Think of it as barristers putting forward their case (argument) in court, where they seek to ensure that the other side has a thorough understanding of their position, which is then reciprocated by the opposing counsel.

Done well, it is where both parties can build trust and develop a new or enhance an existing relationship. It provides each party with the opportunity to outline a clear view on their objectives, how they see the negotiation process progressing, while also enabling them to get a similar reciprocal picture from the other side. The **Preparation** stage will have developed a need to get a greater understanding of the other party's position and this step also provides the other party with the need to get a perspective on your position using well thought out questions. There are three key stages of the **Argue** Step:

- **The opening statement** – a rehearsed statement made at the beginning of the negotiation, which provides the other side a clear view of your position and objective;
- **Effective questioning** – to test your view of the assumptions you've made about the other party's objectives, thinking and position;
- **Effective listening** – hearing what they say, making notes, summarising to ensure understanding and developing more questions to maximise understanding.

Is this the right room for an argument?
– Too much persuasion limits negotiation...

Alan Smith

(Published 5ᵗʰ March 2021)

The word 'argue' conjures up an array of combative, formidable words and typically an energetic use of persuasion, logic and facts to bolster our view of the world, and convince others that not only are we right, but that they must be a fool to think anything else.

Looking at it from a philosophical perspective, Sartre, the great French thinker (the French are after all philosophically superior to the rest of us mortals), said that in the absence of extrinsic meaning, the way we think about how we live our lives becomes the blueprint of our very being.

Anyone who lives differently to us, or thinks differently to us, generates a challenge to our own existence. And is a contest with all that we are.

I think that's what he said. Was a bit too complicated for me to get my head around, to be honest.

If we see winning the argument as the goal for arguing in the first place, perhaps we will generate far more heat than light, and not get beyond the challenges we face. Certainly not as far as we could with a more open approach to the arguing or dialogue process.

A wonderful book, called *Conflicted* by Ian Leslie, talks about the use of 'productive disagreement'.[6] He postulates that in arguments we should strive for a connection with the other side by listening intensely to what they have to say. He says we should be significantly more curious, humorous, aware of how we are coming across and ready to acknowledge our own inadequacies and mistakes.

Using dialogue, we have with others not simply a way to convert, but also a way to absorb and move forward which is a good thing.

There are two ways you might want to think about doing this. First, put yourself in the other party's shoes. If I stood in their role or position, or faced the challenge that they face, how would I behave? You may then see the conflict or misalignment of objectives in a much clearer way.

The second way is to switch off your transmitter and toggle your brain to receive. Ask lots of questions to aid understanding. Even if you disagree with their position at least attempt to understand it, truly understand it.

---

[6] I. Leslie *Conflicted* (2021)

You might not agree with them, but you have a far better chance of finding a compromise if you understand how important it is to them.

Before I began looking into negotiation as a method of resolving conflict, I used to conflate negotiation with persuasion. Now I see the two as close relatives, as we will find ourselves using persuasive language when we negotiate in order to better sell our solutions.

But really negotiation is what we do when overt selling of our position fails.

And you can't argue with that. Oh yes, I can. That's not an argument, that's just a contradiction.

Give to get – When persuasion doesn't work – When it's time to stop selling and start negotiating...

Romana Henry

(Published 24th September 2015)

I go running regularly with a good friend and neighbour who happens to be a criminal defence lawyer. She is married to another lawyer who works in property and estate settlement. On our runs, we exchange tips and advice. She tells me how expensive it would be to divorce my husband, why I shouldn't run a red light and why helping my 17-year-old daughter to obtain fake ID to get into pubs really isn't a good idea. She also tells me why I really must make a will soon, when to put my house on the market and what home improvements not to bother with. In exchange I tell her how to get a better deal in her various negotiations and we regularly brainstorm long lists of things that she would like to get in negotiations in exchange for things she knows she will have to concede. Quite a pair we are. Imagine how much faster we would run if we spoke less and breathed more.

One night on our run, she announced that her brother had just resigned from a high-profile editorial job for a newspaper. He was unhappy with the terms on which the newspaper was willing to let him go. There was a 'non-compete' clause in there whereby he was unable to write on certain subjects for any other publication for 12 months. This, he found, was unacceptable, but he was unable to persuade them why. He spoke to his sister, my jogging pal, and she gave him some second-hand advice. 'Rather than continue to persuade them, why don't you think of something they would really like you to do for them, something you could concede easily but which would be valuable for them, then try to trade this for a shorter 'non-compete' clause.'

He thought about it and came up with an offer to write them a monthly column for six months in exchange for a six-month reduction in his clause. They jumped at the chance and agreed – they were delighted; he was delighted as this was very easy for him to do and would keep his profile high. Win/win.

A couple of days after our run I watched the local news on TV and smiled when I heard the announcement of his resignation.

Persuasion is an important part of the negotiating dialogue and if it works, great! The problem is that we tend to continue to persuade sometimes without realising that it's starting to annoy or entrench the other party. There's an art in recognising when your persuasion is falling on deaf ears and in being prepared to take another tack. I hope I don't need to persuade of you that.

Creativity: It's the future – 'Remember to look at the stars, not down at your feet'

Alan Smith

(Published 15ᵗʰ March 2018)

At the time, I was hugely saddened by the unfortunate demise of Stephen Hawking but massively uplifted not only by his life but by his wonderful approach to it and his ability to live it to the full in what most of us would see as terribly difficult circumstances.

You probably all know his story. Diagnosed with motor neurone disease in 1964 at the tender age of 22, he was given just two years to live. Despite that, not only did he go on to live a full and productive personal life, but he also became a household figure in the world of science and published a best-seller, *A Brief History of Time*.[7] To this day, the book remains a staple of the scientific canon, and its succinct and clear language continues to introduce millions to the universe and its wonders – even I understood about half of it!

Hawking was perhaps most famous for his attempt to discover or identify a set of rules that hold all of science together, a law of everything. 'This complete set of laws can give us the answers to questions like how did the universe begin?' he said. 'Where is it going and will it have an end,

---

[7] S. Hawking *A Brief History of Time* (1989)

[and] if so, how will it end? If we find the answers to these questions, we really shall know the mind of God.' He was notorious for his extraordinary capacity to picture scientific solutions without calculation or experiment.

Pondering, let alone answering questions of this scale, requires any mind to throw out any rule book and think on a different plane.

'*Be curious*'.

Generating the best possible outcome for all at the negotiating table requires an element that you may not initially expect: creativity. This requires thinking 'outside the box' and coming up with new, distinctive solutions to the issues at hand.

Often people see negotiating as a zero-sum game. For me to get what I want, I have to get the other side to give up their share. Now that may work in a simple transactional sense. Do I really care if the company I am trying to buy a TV from gets a worse deal? Not really.

But the reality is in many negotiation scenarios the client or supplier is more than likely to be a long-term partner, and the more effectively we can work together in the long term, the better for me and for them. Creative thinking about where value sits can help enormously in this process before we have the inevitable discussion about how that value is attributed.

'*Intelligence is the ability to adapt to change*'.

In any negotiation, once the true needs have been uncovered for both parties, an option is to involve the other party in a co-operative search for creative options that will drive mutual improvements.

This requires trust, openness and, most important of all, creative thinking.

It may not create a new way of thinking about the universe, but just might help you create a better deal.

(*Quotations* are provided by the great man himself, and wise words for the negotiator. Don't be afraid to aim high, be curious about what things people ask you for and why, and be flexible to adapt to new solutions if change is needed. RIP Stephen Hawking.)

Who needs negotiators when you have processes? – The perils of letting the machines replace the conversation

John McMillan

(Published 23rd November 2017)

A characteristic of business in the UK in recent years, and I suspect in other countries, is the removal of people from the interface between buyer and seller. In the place of the traditional face-to-face meeting is the RFI (Request for Information), the RFP (Request for Proposal) and the E-auction. Indeed, some companies bar any direct communication between the department that has the need and the potential suppliers. As a senior buyer once told me, 'You are interested in relationship selling; we don't want relationships. We are only interested in getting the best deal.'

The techniques that are appropriate when sourcing an engineering component often fail when buying a unique or highly differentiated service. We find that procurement rarely defines the need; they define what they see as the solution and ask the supplier to quote against that. Many years ago, when the British coal industry was nationalised, a buyer from the

National Coal Board (NCB) was visiting a supplier's factory. He saw some state-of-the-art hydraulic pit props, which he had never seen before. He was told that they were for a South African client. He asked why the NCB didn't buy them and was told 'because you never specified them in your order'.

So, my message to procurement is, let those with the need talk to those who might address the need. Yes, you might lose some of your power, but the business will gain overall. And if it is delegated to you, make sure you understand the critical elements of the purchase as opposed to the 'nice to haves'.

Share the purpose of the goods or services you wish to buy with your suppliers and don't just specify your solution. This will allow your suppliers to suggest more innovative and possibly cheaper options.

I wanted to buy a train ticket from Dundee to Glasgow. Instead of just buying the ticket I asked what was the cheapest and was told that if I bought two tickets, one to Perth and another from Perth to Glasgow, I would save 25% of the normal fare without having to leave the train.

Salespeople find it increasingly difficult to get to talk to potential customers. The web has led to the attitude 'if we need you, we'll find you; don't call us, we'll call you'. Procurement is increasingly distanced from those who have the need, often an outsourced function. This means that their understanding of the need is limited and even if they spot an innovative solution, they are rarely empowered to include it because it is 'outside the process'.

If we are to believe the forecasters then computers will replace many of today's jobs, presumably including salespeople and procurement staff. If processes take over from people then we will all lose out. In my selling days I used to say to my clients, 'I know of five different ways to save you money; you only know of one, which is to cut my price.'

And my message for salespeople is to follow the procurement process but also to present your original innovative solution alongside it.

No hard feelings – Good negotiators understand how to manage their behaviour and thus the climate

Alan Smith

(Published 17th March 2016)

Well, there are, actually!

Negotiation involves cold logic, cutting through all the verbiage and careful and clear analysis of the volatile and unpredictable environment before coolly selecting the correct option.

The problem is we rarely get the time, when making the hundreds of decisions we need to make each day in the negotiations that we do, in both our commercial and personal lives. Emotions play a huge part in the actions we take and to some extent the brain's higher function is to sort out many of the choices we have already made and make sense of them after the fact.

A study run in 2015 as part of an MBA course run by Alison Wood Brooks, who is the O'Brien Associate Professor of Business Administration at Harvard, suggests that the outcome of the deals we do will depend to a large extent on the way we deal with our emotions in the cut and thrust of conflict management.[8] The study involved splitting large groups of students and putting them on either side of a conflict. The conflict makes one side the client and the other the supplier in a long-term relationship that has started to go wrong. They need to find a solution that works for both parties and the outcomes could be an amended deal, termination or an expensive legal breakdown. The case is played literally hundreds of times and the outcomes recorded.

In half the cases there is a significant difference in that one side is briefed to act angrily and aggressively for the first 10 minutes before settling down to negotiate. They are asked to blame the other side personally for the problem, interrupt them when they speak, raise their voice and generally be unpleasant (and apparently they really get into it and start questioning parentage, swearing and banging tables, often in wonderfully creative ways!).

After 10 minutes, they calm down and try to reach a settlement.

The results make interesting reading. But are not surprising.

In cases where anger had been deliberately introduced there were significantly fewer deals done, and when deals were reached they were generally much weaker, with significant money being left on the table. No value creation had been explored from either party. Critically, when those deals had been reached the chances of them going to fruition seemed less likely.

---

[8] www.hbs.edu/faculty/Pages/profile.aspx?facId=684820&view=featured-work

What do we learn from this?

Anger, and the potential anger or anxiety response to the other side's anger, is counterproductive.

Now, of course we cannot stop other people from being either genuinely or tactically angry with us, but we can control how we react to it. If the other side does become angry, seek to soothe and assuage, even if you feel the emotion is unwarranted. Perhaps the other thing you should consider is that many negotiations do not complete in one session, and you should manage your time and the process to take the steam out of the emotion and take a break from the table to let things calm down.

You should also build time into preparation to develop your own emotional strategy. Think about how you will react to the other side and their issues and emotions, what you will do if the other side gets angry or anxious.

I know that it is hard to do in this time-pressured commercial world, but it will be time well spent.

Nice but not dim – The perils of losing out by being too agreeable...

Stephen White

(Published 8th March 2018)

If you get time, take a look at the interview of Jordan Peterson by Cathy Newman on Channel 4 News, broadcast in 2018.[9] If you are entertained by intellectual enthusiasm and combative journalism, it will be well worth half an hour of your time.

---

[9] www.channel4.com/news/jordan-peterson-debate-on-the-gender-pay-gap-campus-protests-and-postmodernism (16th January 2018)

Jordan Peterson is the controversial Professor of Psychology at the University of Toronto. After the Channel 4 interview, which has now had over 41 million hits on YouTube alone, his latest book, *12 Rules for Life*, achieved the number one sales spot around the world.[10] Much of the interview is about gender inequality, and particularly the gender pay gap. Peterson doesn't deny that the pay gap exists, but his opinion is that the cause is not simply gender, but rather that it is a melange of many different influences of which gender is one. Another, for example, is 'agreeableness', which includes the traits of being empathic, socially aware, co-operative, un-pushy, relatively selfless and generally 'nice'. People who score high on agreeableness tend to do less well for themselves in corporations; they are promoted more slowly and paid less well than others who display less agreeableness and more 'extraversion', which includes traits of assertiveness and attention seeking. Peterson claims that women have a greater tendency to be agreeable than men and that this is a (non-gender) contributor to what appears to be a gender pay gap.

Which resurrects the evergreen subject – do nice people make less effective negotiators, particularly when negotiating for themselves? It is a question the Scotwork team are frequently asked by course participants – mainly those same nice people who are genuinely worried that they have less competence when dealing with bosses, who by virtue of their seniority already have the balance of power. Sadly, the answer is probably yes, because if they don't put themselves first then nobody else will. And that is where legislation comes in, to

---

[10] J. Peterson *12 Rules for Life* (2019)

level the playing field. Pay gaps should be eliminated when the nice people don't have to negotiate their pay rates because pay equality for all is enshrined in law.

So, I was struck by an article in the *Sunday Times* which revealed that female MPs earn 10.4% less than their male counterparts.[11] Hang on. Surely all MPs earn the same under Equal Pay legislation.

Yes, they do as MPs. But the survey showed that male MPs are more likely to earn more money outside Parliament than women MPs. I suspect this is another manifestation of agreeableness; MPs who do not take extracurricular work believe that morally their parliamentary job should and does occupy all their working time, while those who do outside work claim that they can be a successful MP and still have a few hours spare each week, and that the experience of working in the real world can be useful in their political life as well as earning them a few thousand extra pounds.

People who score highly on agreeableness need some defence mechanisms if they are not to turn into negotiation dimwits. Here are three suggestions:

- **Learn how to tell a good story**. Assertiveness is not about being noisy, it is about weaving a credible narrative that interests and influences the listener. The best storytellers are the world class stand-up comedians – watch a few on YouTube and you will learn and enjoy at the same time.

---

[11] www.thetimes.co.uk/article/revealed-mps-gender-pay-gap-glzhtb0g7

- **Tell them what you want.** If you don't have pay equality and you want it, say so. Don't assume the bosses know you know that inequality exists. Tell them. If pay inequality is embarrassing for the boss, then articulate the demand and force the embarrassment factor up.
- **Find allies, group together and go public.** The power balance in the dispute about whether the BBC bullied presenters into choosing Personal Trading Companies as their vehicle for contracting with the Corporation (and which leaves them facing huge tax demands from HMRC) is significantly changed because 170 of them came together to mount the challenge.

Six-second delay – Taking time under pressure...

Alan Smith

(Published 11th February 2021)

The one thing that you can say about Donald Trump, and let's be honest we could talk for days about his mentality, methods and practice, is that he acts on instinct. Makes decisions fast and is driven principally by his emotions.

In many regards that seems to be why so many Americans love him. I mean, really love him.

He has flown head-buttingly into the face of the weaselly, slimy reputation that many politicians have. Many answer questions with questions, they evade and stick to their own agenda. They filibuster and dance around topics, which leaves many howling at the TV or radio for interviewees to 'answer the flaming question'. They leave the political journalists engaged in a circular, frustrating dilemma of 'do I continue to pursue and get nowhere, or do I move on to their agenda and at least have a discussion?'.

The best politician answer ever is to rebut the question with 'that is an interesting question, but of course the real question you should be concerned with is ...'. Genius to be honest, and the first thing they must teach at Media Training 101.

Trump in contrast tells you what he thinks as soon as he thinks it, if not a bit before.

At least he is not a professional politician, I hear people cry. He talks like us, from the gut.

Acting from the gut has its own problems.

I'm a huge fan of the book *The Chimp Paradox,* written by Professor Steve Peters.[12] The book offers a simple-to-understand exploration of the human psychological condition.

Essentially, Peters suggests we can view the mind as made up of three independent component bits: *the chimp,* the emotional machine that responds rapidly to stimulus, thinks independently of us and can trigger thoughts and feelings that can be either constructive or destructive; *the human,* that rational, analytical part of the brain that processes information in a considered, factual way before eliciting action; and *the computer,* where information including experiences and learned behaviours is stored for future reference.

Now the chimp part (which others may describe as the reptilian part of the brain) acts quickly to get us out of danger. It is unthinking in many respects and instinctive. If you need

---

[12] Prof. S. Peters *The Chimp Paradox* (2012)

to escape a tiger's claws you really don't want anything else on your mind.

I suspect that Trump is the ultimate chimp.

The trouble is most of the time we are now faced with challenges that are less dangerous and possibly more complex. Reining in the chimp is required more often than not and is usually the better solution.

This means we need to engage the higher orders of function, particularly when we are under pressure.

I was listening to the former leader of the Labour Party, Ed Miliband, this week on a podcast. He claimed to have a six-second rule when he was asked a question. He would wait six seconds before giving an answer, allowing his brain to cogitate on the answer before a knee-jerking comeback.

Not sure that works that well on TV or radio, but great advice for the negotiator put under pressure from the other side. Even better, take a summariser to the meeting to buy thinking time.

Give it.

A.

Go.

Answer the question – If only they would listen to and answer the question...

Stephen White

(Published 1st October 2020)

I have many friends who are opinionated, and that is a good thing. Discussing issues of the day with them is always an

interesting experience, because discussion without contro-
versy is deadly boring, and they are far from boring. One of
them has a pet phrase when he disagrees with a POV – 'I hear
what you say,' he says, but what he actually means is, 'You're
wrong'.

The problem with opinionated people is that they hear
but they don't listen. There is a world of scientific difference
between the two. Hearing is a physical process; listening is an
intellectual process. The ancient game of Chinese Whispers
exactly demonstrates this. And so does the modern game
of presidential debates, as illustrated by the tussle between
Trump and Biden in a debate ahead of the 2020 Presidential
election.

Never mind the appalling lack of content, or the dearth of
policy or vision. And never mind the weight of ad hominem
insults and muckraking, much of which was undeserved on
both sides. The fact is that neither man listened to the other,
or to the moderator. They did not answer the questions they
were asked because in many cases the answers would have
been embarrassing for them. They did not respond to points
made by their opponents because they weren't bright enough
or sharp enough to recognise the real issue being raised and
respond to it in a way that was meaningful for the audience.
They just peddled their own premixed cocktail of insults,
half-truths and lies. It was ugly and mean spirited.

Of course, on our side of the pond, we like to think that
we do things differently. Well, to a point, yes, we do, but
different doesn't necessarily mean better. Around the same
time as the presidential debates, Gillian Keegan was Minister
for Apprenticeships and Skills. On the *Today* programme

one morning, she was unable to answer a specific (and quite technical) question relating to regional lockdown restrictions in the north-east of England. Later on that morning, Boris Johnson was unable to answer the same question. Keegan openly admitted that she didn't know the answer to the question posed and spent her airtime telling the audience why she didn't know – because her constituency is in Chichester, not Newcastle. Johnson fudged an answer and then had to admit that he had mis-spoken because the answer he had given was wrong.

If you are struggling to see the connection with the presidential debates, it is this. Both Keegan and Johnson heard the question they were being asked. But they didn't listen to the question. If they had listened, they would have known that the interviewer wasn't interested in the technical lockdown issue. The question was asked to shed light on how the complexity of lockdown restrictions is preventing law-abiding citizens from doing the right thing because they, like the politicians, are confused about what the right thing is. And the most effective response would have been to acknowledge that problem, sympathise and explain.

Negotiators recognise this problem all the time. How often do we remark at the end of a meeting just how many dumb questions 'they' asked? Unsurprisingly, 'they' are saying the same thing about us. The solution is simple curiosity. When you are asked a question, wonder about the motive behind it. Check the motive and then respond to it. You will find that this revelatory experience will make real progress.

These are examples where politicians obfuscate and don't listen and peddle their own responses that bear no relation to the questions asked. Do you think anything is going to change as a result of these recent poor performances on both sides of the Atlantic?

Me neither.

Going through the motions! – Attention and listening gives you an advantage...

Alan Smith

(Published 4th April 2019)

My new dog, Grouse, has been subject to an intense training regime, which has been challenging but is proving to be very successful.

The little blighter has taught me another lesson recently about how just going through the motions is going to bite you back (pun intended) in the long run.

I am doing my best to tire him out and we regularly go out for long walks through the local countryside. I am hitting 25,000 steps a day at least, and sadly the only one getting exhausted is me. Like all good working dogs he is constantly looking for graft and runs from side to side trying to sniff out rabbits, pheasants or any other wild animal he can find.

Lazily, I just let him get on with it. Wandering behind him listening to podcasts. Going through the dog-walk motions so to speak. That is simply not good enough for Grouse. Recognising that I was not engaged, he ran off looking for something more interesting and I lost him for a good 30 minutes. As we were entering spring, many of my local fields were full of pregnant ewes, so my alarm bells and blood pressure all began ringing in my ears. My local farmer, nice bloke though he is, has the right to shoot any dog harassing his flock.

When Grouse eventually returned, I brought him home and called the breeder for some advice. He more or less said what on earth did I expect! It was not the dog's fault, it was mine for not being more actively engaged in what I was doing (to be fair he said it in a much nicer way).

He informed me that when I walk the dog, I have to take a much more active role in keeping his attention, to take a ball and a Gundog dummy to throw, whistle him back to sit and if he gets more than 20 yards away, I have to bring him to heel. Essentially, I have to become the most important thing in his life, all the time.

It made me think about how much distraction there is around us all the time, and how we really need to focus on the job in hand.

Active listening is a much-posited requirement of the great negotiator, and it is one of the things that is being lost in this age of 'over broadcast' communication. Communication is a two-way street and requires our full attention.

We need to respect the other side by paying full attention to what they are saying and show them that we are listening by staying quiet until appropriate, and then summarising accurately what we have heard. We need to provide feedback by being curious about what they are saying (and not saying) and asking lots of questions.

If we really try to understand what is driving the other side and connect with them through appropriate rapport, they may even listen to us in return.

Next time you get the chance to really listen to someone else, do your best to stay with them. You might learn something valuable. I know Grouse taught me something critical this week.

No wonder dogs are our best friends.

Show up and throw up! – Constructive dialogue is more about listening than talking...

Alan Smith

(Published 14th February 2019)

An evocative phrase that I heard in two different settings for the first time last week.

It concerns the behaviour of salespeople who spend inordinate amounts of time in what is best described as rampant persuasion rather than try to understand what the customer wants.

Scotwork are absolute experts in the art of negotiation; we often describe negotiation as what happens when the selling (persuasion) stops.

Truth is that many of the skills of the excellent negotiator are complementary to the skills exhibited by the proficient salesperson.

I had been asked to present on a platform for a client's sales conference, giving a few insights into negotiation for a crowd about to undertake our Advancing Negotiation Skills course.

Before I was on stage, I heard the sales director ask the group if any of them had heard of Graham Westport, as

Westport had provided the best lesson in sales that the afore-mentioned director had ever received.

Not one hand went up, which was just as well because Westport was a potential buyer for the young sales director on his way up the corporate ladder.

The salesman put in a cold call to Westport in an attempt to present his company's wares and unusually he was put straight through! In shock, the young salesman went into his patter about what his company could do, how big they were, what their area of specialism was, etc, etc.

Westport allowed him to 'drone on', his words, not mine, for 60 seconds before delivering the best lesson in the young man's sales life.

He said to him that he had just listened to a 60-second broadcast about something that was not relevant, not important and certainly not persuasive. The salesman knew nothing about his company (and seemed pretty sketchy about his own organisation) and had wasted both of their time.

The good salesperson knows that curiosity and doing your homework are critical to getting interest from the other side. Dale Carnegie said you can gain more influence by being interested in the other party for 10 minutes than you can in getting them to be interested in you for 10 months.

The salesperson should know this, the negotiator must.

Negotiation requires us to deeply understand the other side, and in a world of information overload, we should do our homework; in a world of abundant technology, this is inexcusable.

But nothing beats the face-to-face time of asking lots of questions, which ironically is the most persuasive thing of all we can do.

Finding out what the other side wants and how badly they want it allows us to create deals that will live in the real world. That is what showing up should be about.

THE 8-STEPS

CHAPTER 3

READING AND RESPONDING TO SIGNALS

As negotiations develop, even in the most collaborative scenarios, people can become entrenched in their commitment to intractable decisions or demonstrate inflexibility. Humans are competitive and this can lead to making what we call absolute statements, where they take seemingly fixed positions.

You can expect a change in language to qualified statements as the negotiation develops, which can be associated with increased flexibility. This can also be characterised by the other party asking questions about a previously intractable issue, which typically signals flexibility.

As well as tone and approach, their posture and the language can help you to understand their true feelings on an issue.

Signals are welcome and they indicate flexibility. It's important to be alert and recognise them. Crucially, build trust **reward** signals – don't punish them.

It's only words... – The importance of non-verbal communication...

David Bannister

(Published 26th March 2020)

As I sit here in the third week of self-isolation – the first two having been forced on me because I holidayed for three weeks in Thailand – I have reflected on how important social interaction is to us all. I can't cuddle my new grandson or play games with my other grandchildren, and I am maintaining social distance from neighbours although, to be honest, where one of them is concerned that represents no change from the norm!

I suppose that we may consider ourselves lucky that in the days of email, social media and Skype, we are not as isolated as the transatlantic rowers who now seem to crowd my timeline with advice based on their solitary experiences. I gave some thought, though, to what this might mean for negotiators. For negotiation still goes on in this strange new world we now occupy. The business my wife works for has been contracting with the government to help with projects associated with its response to Covid, while their huge office in London's Docklands is deserted. Issues have to be addressed and agreements have to be reached, often in very short times-cales. I was reminded recently in writing a piece for a client about the work in the 1970s of Professor Albert Mehrabian who suggested that the fact of removing the element of direct interaction between humans when they communicate presents a new problem.[13] Mehrabian postulated that communication was about the words we use, the voice and tone with which we say them and the body language that accompanies them. He suggested the following proportions:

- Words 7%;
- Voice and tone 38%;
- Body language 55%.

These figures have been contested many times and the good professor himself had cause to modify and suggested that it depended, as everything does, on the situation. Nevertheless, I recall watching one of my own consulting team years ago proving the point to a group on a training programme. She stood on a chair and told her audience of about 30 students to do what she *told* them to do. She then put her index finger on her head and said, 'Put your finger on your head', and they did so. She gave several more of these commands and her actions were followed carefully by the students. Then she told them to put their finger on their nose while she put hers on her chin. About 8 out of 10 of the class ignored what she had clearly told them to do and also reached for their chin! The moral of this story? Gestures are so important to our understanding of what words we are using to discuss. Mehrabian suggested that we

---

[13] www.bl.uk/people/albert-mehrabian

will usually believe what we see more than what we hear. Not convinced? Try to imagine someone telling you they would trust you with absolutely anything while not maintaining any eye contact. Do you believe the words or the eyes? Yes, me too.

When life was 'normal' we at Scotwork always told people that as negotiators they had to work hard to ensure an understanding of everything they say, and also that they had to strive to ensure absolute comprehension of what others say to them. Now, it is even more important than ever – we will be under pressure to move things on quickly in the face of the dynamics of this new reality. We will make mistakes because we have had part of the process of comprehension removed from us. Mistakes take time to rectify and time is something we have not got in abundance, especially for those who are on the 'front line'. So remember, a little time spent testing understanding, clarifying and reflecting now, even under real pressure, may save vital time in the future.

Be well and safe.

Unconscious bias – It's still out there, we're all still susceptible...

Stephen White

(Published 18ᵗʰ February 2021)

Bill Michael, the CEO of one of the leading accounting/consulting firms in the UK, fell on his sword after a video clip was circulated on social media. The video shows him responding robustly at a meeting with some of his senior colleagues to their various complaints. Amongst other comments he tells them not to play the victim card (they were complaining about falling bonuses and pension contributions) and he denies the existence of unconscious bias ('utter crap'), citing as evidence that whenever unconscious bias training has been conducted by the firm, nothing subsequently changes.

Unconscious bias is defined as underlying attitudes and stereotypes that people unconsciously attribute to another person or group of people that affect how they understand and engage with a person or group. It is interesting that many of the newspaper reports about Michael's fall from grace start off by describing him as 'Australian Bill Michael', in itself encouraging a form of bias. That he is Australian leads us to a view about his personality – Australian stereotypes are, according to a quick internet search, 'sporty, outdoors-loving, down to earth, hard-drinking, funny, surfers'. According to reports, Michael does exhibit one or more of these traits (so what?), but unconscious bias goes much further than identification. It predicts that liking one or more of these traits might cause people to be biased subconsciously towards anyone who shares them – a candidate in a recruitment exercise, a potential partner, a client, a supplier.

We would like to think that societal changes over the last 50 years mean that most examples of conscious bias have been eradicated, or at least driven underground. Read the classified column of a provincial newspaper from the 1950s and you will see adverts for flats and bedsits to rent or for jobs with the phrase 'No blacks', 'No Jews' or 'Irish need not apply' listed alongside the stipulation 'No dogs'. Advertisers would be breaking the law if they did that today, but similar statements still proliferate ('No DSS'). Unconscious bias is more sinister. It is never signalled, never advertised and often never even acknowledged by the holder, but it is still there.

In conflict situations, unconscious bias is a major problem. An example of this is in the selection of jury members. Theoretically, the first 12 qualified people to be eligible for service from this week's list should be as good as any other selection. But defence counsels know that some jurors will have unconscious bias for or against their client, and sometimes – particularly in the US – a large amount of background research is done before the selection of jury members is made. In some judicial settings there is scope for many jurors to be rejected in order for the defence to get those it thinks will be most sympathetic towards their client. To get a flavour of this read John Grisham's novel *The Runaway Jury* or watch the 2003 film of the book staring Gene Hackman.[14]

In his book *How to Argue and Win Every Time*, lawyer Gerry Spence likens unconscious bias, by definition, to prejudice, and he uses this similarity to explore the issue of effective argument.[15] An example he uses is that of the 'preacher' – any man or woman of the cloth. He suggests that preachers are more likely to support capital punishment – an eye for an eye, a tooth for a tooth, and therefore, by extension, a life for a life – than the average citizen. Very important for a defence counsel to know this in a murder trial where manslaughter is an optional outcome – defence counsel wouldn't want a preacher on that jury!

---

[14] J. Grisham *The Runaway Jury* (1996); 20th Century Fox *Runaway Jury* film (2003)

[15] G. Spence *How to Argue and Win Every Time* (1996)

Similarly, knowing and understanding the biases of the counterparty in a negotiation can be an important element in the achievement of a deal. Knowing (or guessing) the biases of the individual enables the construction of arguments that will be more sympathetically received. Knowing that you share an interest in a sport, or hobby, or hail from the same place or follow the same team might make the difference between diffidence (I don't care whether we do a deal or not) and resolution (OK, because it's you, let's do it).

One practical result of corporate concerns about unconscious bias is the increasing phenomenon of the dehumanisation of process; the theory that if a piece of work can be done robotically then the possible effects of bias are eliminated. Hence the growth of the 'RFP' (request for proposal) culture within procurement. The buyer that doesn't ever meet a seller can't exert bias.

Or can they? I suspect that if you analysed the questions that sellers are asked to answer in a typical RFP (for example, where is your head office? What were your last five years' profits? Name three current clients. Give a profile of your consultants), you might find fertile ground for unconscious bias in the mind of the RFP compiler. Food for thought.

An opinion-free blog – Saying it doesn't make it true...

Stephen White

(Published 24th September 2020)

Over the years I have spent quite a lot of time in Bradford. My wife, at that time my girlfriend, went to Margaret McMillan

College of Education in the town. We were regular visitors to the Alhambra Theatre, and later on, I taught numerous managers working for Grattan's, the mail order catalogue company. It is a fine town, populated by great characters.

In 1981, Bradford made headlines when it declared itself to be a nuclear-free zone. No one quite understood what that meant in practice, but the literal interpretation was that if there was a nuclear war Bradford wasn't going to be involved, and any foreign enemy aiming missiles at the UK had therefore to ensure that they avoided hitting Bradford. We all wondered if Russia had quite understood. In the end, nuclear-free status did not happen.

They were at it again in 2014, when George Galloway declared Bradford an Israel-free zone, telling locals to boycott Israeli-made products. This time the plan came unstuck because most people didn't care enough to take any action, but if they had they would have found that products designed, developed or made in Israel included USB memory sticks, the Intel chips used in most mobile phones and laptops, and parts of Google's technology, which the good people of Bradford would probably have objected to doing without. In the end, Israel-free status did not happen.

I was reminded of these two events by a news item reporting that approximately 100 religiously conservative Polish local authorities have declared themselves LGBT-free zones. Intellectually, this means that they deny LGBT perspectives; in practice it means that they adopt generally homophobic attitudes at official levels, including, for example, banning Gay Pride marches and demonstrations, and possibly discriminating against LGBT individuals, perhaps expecting them to change to what they believe is 'normal' orientation, or at least persuading them to leave town.

I expect they will fail, just as Bradford did. The problem is that whatever they declare, peoples' sexuality and gender choices are neither created by official decree nor eliminated by them. Add to that the increasing ire of the EU, which can wield some major sanctions on Poland if they choose. I expect that the LBGT-free declarations will evaporate (although, unfortunately, the discrimination will not).

Saying that something will happen does not make it happen. Boris Johnson has found this out over the last six months in his pronouncements on Brexit (oven-ready deal) and Covid (all over by Christmas) and lots more. Untrue statements made in the guise of confidence boosters always get found out, and even if the motive was benign, the effect is ultimately negative.

Think about that next time you are inclined to bluster about the certainty of an event which is by no means certain during a negotiation, or you hear it from your negotiating partner. If you can predict the nonsensicality then rather than just argue, trade the opinion. For example, the people of Bradford might have said to their councillors, 'To be a nuclear-free zone you need to get Russia on side. Prove that you have done that, and we will support you. Fail and we require you all to resign for being bonkers.'

That would have sorted the men from the boys (sorry, I meant the adults from the children).

Mind your language! – Listen carefully, the subtleties are important...

Romana Henry

(Published 21ˢᵗ May 2021)

I love language. It's my thing, has been since I was a kid. Hopeless at math or science but oh how I love language. My maternal grandparents came to Scotland penniless between the wars, opened a 'Gelateria' and made the most delicious ice cream and enough money to have their six children educated privately! Rather than 'Macari's' ice cream shop, they had to name it 'The Soda Fountain', as when WW2 hit the 'Tallys', as we were known, were not always in favour with the Scots thanks to Mussolini, and Italian shops were vandalised on a regular basis. My Nonno was whipped away to a prisoner of war camp on the Isle of Man for two years (he loved the island!) leaving Nonna to fend for herself and look after the family.

As well as attending a regular school, my brother and I were sent to an Italian school on a Saturday morning. I loved it. We learned Italian through songs, poems, games and having fun – best way to learn. Every summer, we went on three-week language holidays to Viareggio in Tuscany, with other 'Italo-Scozzesi' kids, trips heavily subsidised by the Italian government in a bid to keep the language alive in Scotland. Brilliant idea and what was not to like! Language classes in the morning, beach in the afternoon, and in the evening, we mixed with the locals to practise the language. And the food, what can I say. Anyway, I was fluent in Italian by the time I reached high school and a passion for language was born and continues to this day.

I was recently on holiday in Portknockie, a tiny fishing village in north-east Scotland where my paternal grand-mother was born, next to Cullen, where the famous soup 'Cullen Skink' originates (smoked haddock with tatties (pota-toes), onions and milk (not double cream, by the way, that's as bad as putting ice in single malt whisky)). Try Cullen Skink if you haven't, it's delicious, nutritious and easy to make; let me know what you think.[16] There are public toilets in Cullen that display signs above them as 'Loons' (boys) and 'Quines' (girls). The kids are taught 'proper' English in school but as soon as the bell rings they revert to their own dialect, Doric. Let me give you some examples:

- 'Fit like?' is 'How are you?';
- 'Far ee gan' is 'Where are you going?';
- 'I'm awa fer a dook in ma dookers' is 'I'm off for a swim in my swimsuit';
- 'Far dive ee bide?' is 'Where do you live?';
- 'He's an affa feel loon' is 'He's a naughty/horrid boy';
- 'Yer sheen are full' is 'Your shoes are dirty'.

Scotwork's HQ is in Glasgow, where they also have a language of their own. A couple of years ago a colleague used a phrase that baffled me. She said, 'Sometimes you have to bum your own chuff.' I had to ask her to repeat (I'm from Edinburgh!), and even then was clueless. I had visions of hair removal devices and other things which make the eyes water.

---

[16] www.thespruceeats.com/traditional-scottish-cullen-skink-re-cipie-435379

It transpires that 'bum yer own chuff' means 'blow your own trumpet'. Who knew! I love it, it sounds so irreverent.

Language in any negotiation is important and must be carefully planned in each step of the process. From preparation, where you should be deciding exactly what you will say to open the meeting, what questions you'll be asking, what information you'll be giving, right through to the words you use to close the meeting and ensure nothing else will be asked of you, and that everything is agreed and can be implemented by both parties.

Throughout the entire process, we give and receive verbal signals that we must be aware of as they can often show flexibility around what's being said. For example, how many signals are there in the following phrase? Imagine the other party, in response to my proposal, says, 'That is difficult for me to agree today'. There are four potential signals in the phrase:

- That – is there something else that you could agree to, if not that?;
- Difficult – what would I have to do to make that easier for you to agree to today?;
- Me – would someone else be able to agree to it?; and
- Today – when would you be able to agree to that?

Listen carefully for those signals and then test them with good questions.

You should be very aware of the language you use. If you tell me that you are here to increase my price by 'something in the region of, or around about, or more or less 5%', then please do not expect me to agree to anything near 5%; far less is what you have signalled that you will settle for so that's what you are likely to get. We give signals all the time: fine if that's your intention, if it's not, then don't give them and use definitive language instead.

Arrivederci. In bocca al lupo!!

Haircut 101 – The same approach won't work in every situation...

Stephen White

(Published 11th February 2016)

When I had a haircut, I learned something simple but useful. Chatting to the barber, I asked if he had ever been to a particular local restaurant. Yes, he said, but it was about five years ago and it wasn't very good. He had found a small piece of plastic in his mouth while eating his meal, and he was unimpressed with the response from the waiter. He explained.

'I said to him, I am not complaining or making a fuss, because I am not that kind of person, but I think you should know that this piece of plastic was in my food.' The waiter looked at it and said, 'Cool, man. Thanks for telling me,' and wandered off. No apology, no compensation or anything like that. I was seething inside. So I haven't been back to that restaurant since then,' said my barber.

There is some cognitive dissonance here. My barber was irritated because he didn't get an apology and/or some compensation. But by framing his comments to the waiter as *not* a complaint he was effectively saying that he didn't want either an apology or compensation. His outward laid-back approach hid his true emotional state, unfortunately to his detriment.

There are probably some cultural overtones here. Most north-western Europeans don't become outwardly emotional when something goes wrong. They understate the problem, they don't ask for a remedy, and so normally they don't get what they hoped for in return. But their outward behaviour often masks an emotional state of mind. Just calling the waiter over to say something negative will be emotionally uncomfortable in itself.

I recently rented a car from Avis. The clerk told me he was giving me a free upgrade to a bigger car, which was a station wagon. I told him I didn't want a bigger car or a station wagon – I had specifically booked a small car because parking in the city I was in is a nightmare so the smaller the car, the better. He persevered. I stayed calm and said no again. He said he didn't have a smaller car immediately available; I would have to wait. I politely waved my preferred-status card to try to intimidate him. It failed. Needing to get to my business meeting I capitulated.

But imagine if, while I was being very calm, I could overhear a similar conversation at the next counter where that customer kicked up such a fuss that it was the clerk who gave in, rather than the customer, and a smaller car became instantly available. Would that change my behaviour? Would I become more outwardly emotional? I think it would.

My point is not that emotional behaviour always gets better deals, but rather that being able to change the placidity or noisiness of approach is built into all of us, and we should encourage our outward emotions to vary according to the outcome which will result. If noisier behaviour produces a better deal, be noisy!

Liar, liar, pants on fire – Some words of caution about lying in negotiation...

Alan Smith

(Published 17th December 2015)

Is there a difference between telling lies and just being misleading?

I guess lying, rather like beauty, may be in the eye of the beholder.

'I want you to listen to me. I'm going to say this again – I did not have sexual relations with that woman, Miss Lewinsky.'

Was this the most blatant lie in modern times? Or had Bill Clinton somehow convinced himself, when he uttered those memorable words in 1998, that his physical relationship with Monica Lewinsky did not constitute 'sexual relations'?

Even if we grant that generous interpretation, his proclamation was, according to any usual understanding of 'sexual relations', certainly misleading.

Historically, if a politician is caught in an outright lie – claiming something to be true which he or she knows to be false – it can be political suicide. At the very least it can prove highly damaging. In recent years, this has become less the case.

The practice of misleading often works through what philosophers call 'conversational implicature'. When we communicate with one another, there are a set of background rules that govern the meaning of our sentences.

An example: 'We want you to drop your price as you are certainly not the cheapest option.' The suggestion being that the best price may be the selection criterion. However, as most of would recognise, that may not be the case.

In the cut and thrust of negotiations, being misleading and even lying seems to be common. We see it in the classroom all the time, despite the fact that people are being filmed often and recognise that their lies will be named and shamed.

Indeed, most negotiators accept that lying and misleading are part of the game. A study at Kellogg Business School asked groups if they felt they had been lied to in a negotiation – 40% said yes.[17] Twenty per cent said that they regularly lied to gain advantage – I think that they were lying!

So what do we do?

Well, be careful about deliberately lying or being misleading. If you get caught out, rather like the disgraced politician, you may never be trusted again.

If you feel you are being lied to, check to see whether the behaviour is consistent with the lie. If they say that all your competitors are cheaper for the same quality and service, why are they even talking to you?

There is either some other source of power they are misleading you about, or just a good old-fashioned lie has been outed.

---

[17] www.kellogg.northwestern.edu/news_articles/2014/05122014-negotiation_lies.aspx

THE 8-STEPS

CHAPTER 4

CREATING MOMENTUM THROUGH PROPOSALS

M aking a proposal is the best way to move the negotiation forward. In the **Argue** Step, people often
continue to try to force the other party to see the world the
way they see it, which then moves to persuasion that often
leads to point-scoring and circular arguments, and results in
the negotiation getting stuck in its tracks.

One way to avoid this malaise is to either make or invite
a proposal (with a strong preference for the former). Think
of a negotiation as climbing a mountain; there are times
for pausing and reflection – where am I, where is the other
party and what do I need to do next – and there are times
to create momentum and making a proposal is the best way
to achieve this. It is our strong belief that any proposal you

make should be realistic, where it addresses all the issues discussed, is credible in that it's supported by the facts, and is at the other party's limit according to your understanding (or, if unknown, the high point of your intended position). You will see from the stories in this book numerous examples of the importance of making a proposal as it sets the agenda and shifts the focus of the negotiation to your perspective; simply put, a proposal beats an argument.

When receiving a proposal, always probe the basis of it. There are a number of ways to respond, including adjournment, making an instant counterproposal, and best of all by making a considered counterproposal where you build on the other party's proposal.

There are two fundamental styles of negotiation, **competitive** (adversarial) and **co-operative** (collaborative). The factors that influence **competitive** negotiation are one-off transactions, where the relationship has been mandated, there are low levels of trust, emotions often run high and the outcomes are *win-lose*, which often results in value erosion. **Co-operative** negotiations are typified by long-term voluntary relationships, trust, tolerance and understanding of the other party's position, and are where skilled negotiators like to play and drive *win-win* (value creation) outcomes.

Bad golf – The power of a proposal...

Romana Henry

(Published 14th May 2021)

Golfing (badly) with my chum one Sunday evening, I asked what the week ahead at work held for her. She works for a charity that looks after children with severe autism, their parents, and carers, providing them with vital respite, amongst other things. They, like all charities, had a terrible year through the pandemic, not only with the lack of donations and funding but due to staffing issues, with sickness and people self-isolating resulting in many parents and carers not getting the much-needed support this charity provides.

She explained that as we came out of lockdown, while some people will continue to work from home, at least part-time, others must be physically in the offices which are situated near the children's residences. The charity is amalgamating various offices into one central office, so they need a larger office. They looked around for months but found nothing to suit in the right location. They had the option of staying where they were, in an industrial estate, which is made up of various offices of different sizes, but moving into larger offices that were now empty in the estate seemed to be a possible solution. My friend was planning to talk to the owners to see how much more they would charge for the larger offices.

Wait a minute, who has the power here? The property owners will surely be keen to keep my friend's business and the rental income, given the other offices have been vacated and are lying empty and costing them money. The country is awash with empty commercial properties, so the power is surely in the hands of those looking to rent. I think there's a deal to be done here. All this as I was pitching onto the fourth green.

Don't ask them to make you a proposal, you make the proposal yourself. Tell them you are looking to move to a larger (but no more expensive) office and that there are lots of options available to you. Tell them you want the larger office but can't pay more than the current rent. Unrealistic – I don't think so. Ballsy? Perhaps, but you don't ask, you don't get. What's the worst that could happen? They say 'no'. If so, no harm done. 'No' is only the starting point of most negotiations anyhow. I presented three options to my friend (and missed my birdie putt):

- You try to persuade them and play the 'pandemic-no budget-we're a charity' card (emotional blackmail if you prefer, but worth a try);
- You ask some great open-ended questions and listen carefully to the response – perhaps you can problem-solve a mutually beneficial and low-cost solution; or
- You negotiate – you are going to have to trade something back to them to get what you want. Not knowing that much about the variables potentially involved in this negotiation I suggested using one of the most common and easily applicable ones – time. How long is your lease normally? One year. Could you extend this? Yes, possibly. When do you pay the rent? Monthly. Could you pay three months upfront? Possibly. What would you really love to have? Free use of additional meeting rooms. OK, so here's the next proposal you make: 'If you agree to give us the larger office at the same price as the smaller office, then we

will sign an 18-month lease rather than a one-year lease'. They say 'two years' for the lease. Close the deal by asking for either free use of meeting rooms once a month, a couple of extra car parking spaces or use of the storage shed outside, or bike racks, or whatever non-contentious things you could get which are of value to you but low cost to them. This additional request should compensate your move from 18 months to two years of lease.

Three points to note in this blog:

- As negotiators, we often underestimate the power we have, or indeed we don't stop to think about where the power lies and how we can best exploit it. Before any negotiation, part of your preparation should involve analysing the power balance by asking yourself this: what do we have that they want and that they want to avoid, and what do they have that we want and that we want to avoid;
- The power of a proposal – you be the one to make the first proposal if you know what you want. Be bold but realistic, and be prepared for initial rejection with various options to counter; and
- If you're playing golf, concentrate on your golf and keep the smarty pants advice until you're at the 19th hole. I went around the course that day 12 shots over my handicap and lost three balls!

Open buying – Develop alternative (creative) strategies in your negotiations...

Stephen White

(Published 13th September 2018)

People are fascinated by pound shops. They've been around the high street for many years. Stores like Poundland, Poundstretcher, Poundworld and others grew their estate and their customer numbers rapidly when Woolworths failed and austerity kicked in at the beginning of 2009. Not all have succeeded. The 99p Stores were absorbed into Poundland, and Poundworld went into administration. For most, the original premise – that everything in the store is £1 – has had to go as inflation limits the stock range that can be sold profitably at that price point.

Most of us like a bargain, so most of us have shopped in one or other of these stores from time to time and wondered just how they were able to sell seven-piece screwdriver sets, mega-sized bags of biscuits and multipacks of batteries for only £1 each. TV programmes like *Saving Poundstretcher* broadcast on Channel 4 are irresistible for their car-crash spectacle.

One successful player in the market is T J Morris Ltd, trading as Home Bargains. With over 400 stores turning over £2 billion, the Home Bargains formula obviously works. Part of the success is down to their buying policy, which they call 'open buying'. On specific days any prospective supplier can go to their head office in Liverpool and show their wares to a member of the buying team. They get an instantaneous decision. But there is a rule. If you pitch your price and the buyer says 'no', that's it. No second chance. No haggling. No negotiation. No sale.

So suppliers conclude that the only rational strategy is to offer their lowest price straight away and hope that it is low enough to get a 'yes'. This means that they make their margin razor thin, and it gives Home Bargains the opportunity to buy more cheaply than their competitors.

But I heard an anecdote last week, tittle-tattle but probably with some foundation, that turns this strategy on its head. The story is that a wholesaler specialising in one of the categories Home Bargains sells bought a large consignment of branded goods from a manufacturer not normally seen in discount stores at an exceptionally good price because they were 'last year's design'. The supplier had no idea how to price the goods and ensure success. He decided to go to a T J Morris's open 'buying day' and met a buyer. He gave the buyer the manufacturer's invoice for the goods and offered to sell for that price plus whatever the buyer felt was a reasonable commission. The buyer gave him an instant decision: Yes, he would take the goods, and he would pay the wholesaler 10% commission – way more margin than the wholesaler would have added if he had decided to pitch a price.

In the version of the story, I was told the buyer was Mr Morris himself, who is very much hands-on in the business. Maybe that made a difference. There are two lessons from this tale. First, when there appears to be only one sensible way to behave, think outside of the box – there are always other options. Second, where there is a lack of market information it may be better to play the odds and let the other side go first.

Inside room only... – You can always get what you want...

Horace McDonald

(Published 8ᵗʰ September 2022)

One of the great things about running negotiation training courses is meeting a variety of people from many different industries and cultures and sometimes making long-term friends. When asking participants about their personal interests, travel always features highly. Strangely though, not for me. I have travelled extensively on business, mostly in Europe and the US, and spent a year in Germany as a student and an intern in the early 1980s. Don't get me wrong, I like a nice holiday, but I get bored with anything more than a couple of weeks and the idea of discovering remote parts of the world fills me with dread. Only recently have I tried to understand why this is the case, and I've attributed it partly to my ethnicity.

Some of my reticence to travel was developed in my formative years. At the age of nine I was taken to Jamaica by my father for six weeks as my parents were considering moving the whole family back there. Despite having been their first child born in the UK, I was transplanted from south London to the Jamaican countryside to live with my grandparents. It was quite a contrast and I remember getting huge boils on my skin (possibly from the change in food/ environment) and seeing decapitated chickens running around before they passed out and were then plucked for that evening's dinner.

However, I think the more relevant factor in my reluctance to travel is that I grew up in the 1970s and 1980s when going abroad was very expensive (holidays were beyond the reach of my family) and many parts of the world were not welcoming to people of colour, particularly my colour. This has undeniably improved over recent years, but a recent trip to Lisbon with my wife and daughter suggests that problems still remain. I like Portugal, partly because many people of colour live there. One night we decided to have a meal at a restaurant in a golf/tennis complex where my daughter and I had played tennis and I'd enjoyed coffee earlier in the week with my wife, served by a delightful waitress. It was a lovely warm evening and as we approached the maître d' station, a black family was waiting in front of us. Despite there being plenty of available tables outside, the maître d' immediately proposed that they sit inside, and led them to an indoor table. At this point, it became immediately clear to me what was going on... The maître d' turned next to me, saying 'you would like a table inside'. This was not a question, but a statement - one which I immediately rebuffed, insisting on being seated outside, which they agreed to.

Later, my wife came back livid from a bathroom break as she had noticed that the majority of people dining inside the restaurant were black, and you won't be surprised to hear that my daughter and I were the only people of colour sitting outside.

There are a few things at play here that pertain to negotiation. Getting your proposal on the table focuses the negotiation on your needs and shifts the balance of power to you. What the other family failed to understand is that they were in a negotiation and, as is often the case, underestimated the power they had. Even *if* they did want to sit inside, they were not given the choice! If you don't ask for what you want, you won't get it. If you don't like what you're offered, say *no* and tell the other side what you want. Failing to do that as a negotiator means you will lose out, and in this case, further entrench the almost certain bias at play.

There's never anything on anyway – If you don't ask, you don't get...

Alan Smith

(Published 4th June 2015)

A relatively small and parochial point, but it illustrates that opportunities to negotiate abound. A deal may just improve your position in any walk of life.

I'd flown into JFK on a business trip with the intention of staying in Manhattan on Monday prior to starting work on Tuesday, and had booked into a small hotel just off Broadway.

Now, New York is five hours behind UK time so at around 9.00pm (2.00am on my body clock) I decided to turn in.

I switched on the TV for a little R & R (rest and recuperation). Nothing doing, intermittent picture and no sound. I called down to reception. A knock on the door.

The technical guy managed to fix the TV. Problem solved.

After a couple of hours of fitful sleep, I came round at 4.00am local time, groggy and grumpy.

I switched on the TV. Nothing. Problem back.

It crossed my mind to get the technical guy back. But at 4.00am? Not very happy. One of my priorities when staying in a hotel with the possibility of jet lag is having a decent entertainment system.

At reception that morning I informed the desk about the problem.

They wisely apologised and asked me what they could do to fix the problem that they had created. A great question.

Now, tempting as it was to have a good old rant and complain – not much sleep makes anyone grumpy – I resisted. I also recognised a deal opportunity. I made a proposal: upgrade me to a better room and give me a free movie – and that would make the problem go away. Deal done.

Look, the reality of life is that things go wrong. Mistakes get made. Stuff breaks. Changes create hassle. Having a good old moan is an option, but it gets you very little apart from the pleasure in making someone else unhappy and an increase in blood pressure.

If you have a complaint, make a proposal to improve your position. It just might work.

Strictly come negotiating – Dancing to the beat of a better deal...

David Bannister

(Published 3rd December 2015)

Here in the UK (and in many parts of the world) in the autumn and the first part of our winter, a televisual phenomenon hits our screens on a Saturday night. It's called *Strictly Come Dancing*, or just *Strictly* to the real addicts. A number of so-called celebrities are partnered with professional dancers and week by week they compete against each other in a knockout competition where viewers' votes decide which contestant will be eliminated each week. Millions of eager followers tune in to this programme in the months it is on our televisions. I am not usually one of them, but my wife is an aficionado. So I find other things to do when this programme is on. Except for a little bit of the programme this year when Jane, my wife, calls me and says, 'Katie's dancing!'. This refers to one of this year's contestants, Katie Derham, who I really want to win (and so do lots of others, some because she is partnered with a male dancer of great good humour and demeanour who has never managed to progress far in the contest).

Derham first came to the TV screens for most of us when she became the youngest newscaster on British television at the age of 27 (she is now 45). Since then, she has broadened her career in radio and on television and presents programmes of classical music in both media. She is remembered by some for the way in which, at age 27, she was attacked verbally by some older and more established television figures who did not seem to be in favour of young (and let's be honest, attractive) people broadcasting the television news bulletins. One of them somewhat uncharitably remarked that you didn't need to be intelligent to read the news from a teleprompter – he went on to suggest that the substantial salary associated with these over-rated talents was not merited either.

Why do I tell you all of this? Well, the salary that Derham was paid was never, to my knowledge, a matter of public record, although newspapers following the tirades from the grumpy old (usually men) complainers set her income variously at between £125,000 and £250,000 back in the 1990s. What she was paid is not material here; the manner in which she achieved it is. In a recent newspaper article recording an interview with her, Derham was inevitably asked about that 'huge' salary. She said to her interviewer that when she was asked to move from minority interest programmes to the high-profile newsreader role, she had to decide what sort of salary package to ask for. She pointed out that there were no published salary rates for such positions and that there was no known precedent or job evaluation on which she was able to base any claim for her pay. So, how to pitch her position in this important negotiation? Simple, said Derham, you consider what you think you are worth to the potential employer – how much they want you, how good you will be at the job, what you might do for the viewer ratings, and you pitch your salary proposal accordingly. Evidently, she did get a deal she found acceptable and read the news for some years on two networks.

The lesson for me here is a simple one for the negotiator: when you make a proposal, consider what you want, marshall your supporting arguments and facts should you need to use them and *say* what you want. No doubt there were other features to the deal done – everything these days from contract length to image rights – and no doubt elements of these will have formed her wish list, but the key decision is 'what am I worth and how badly do they want me to do the job?'. That determines your negotiating position and gives you power to bargain. It seems that Derham may be almost as accomplished in negotiating as she is in dancing the tango – almost! Roll on Saturday night!

Tell them what you want – Take advantage by making your proposal first...

Robin Copland

(Published 31st October 2019)

Negotiations are often formulaic. Management, for example, go into a negotiation fully expecting the union to make the first proposal. This approach has been accepted as the norm for so many years that somehow it is seen as 'not the done thing' to do anything different. If management is keen to put a radical new proposition on the table, then 'waiting for the union to make the first proposal' is obviously silly, but it's amazing how often negotiators blindly follow procedure and do just that.

I have often heard it said – and typically at drinks parties when someone finds out what I do for a living! – that the secret of great negotiators is 'never to tell people what you really want'. So let's take the combination of these two techniques – 'letting the other side lead with their proposal as a matter of course', and 'never letting the other side know what you want' and see what happens.

Party One: 'Make me an offer.'

Party Two: 'No.'

Party One: 'Oh – go on.'

Party Two: 'No.'

Party One: 'No, really. Make me a very generous offer that meets all my needs and expectations.'

Party Two: 'Which bit of "no" was it that you weren't getting? Your proposal is outrageous.'

Party One: 'But I haven't made a proposal.'
Party Two: 'Exactly. And the answer's still "no".'

I'm a great believer in being transparent about my expectations during a meeting. The earlier I can communicate to
the other side what it is that I want, the more time the other
side has to work out the circumstances in which they can give
me just that. This is especially true when what I want is either
controversial or a long way removed from the status quo.

In these kinds of circumstances, it becomes really
important to be absolutely specific about exactly what it is
that I need. Are there any exceptions to that basic rule – tell
people what you want? There are maybe a few.

For instance, if you genuinely do not know what it is that
you want, for example, someone comes to you with a new
product or solution to a problem.

Another example is where you think that if you let the
other side lead, they may come up with a deal that is better
than the one you would have asked for (though the chances
of that happening are maybe not as high as you think!).

Or someone makes a complaint about a product or
service that you have provided and that has gone wrong. Let
them tell you the level of compensation that they want – most
of the time, they haven't a clue!

But generally, telling the other side what you want is the
way forward. Constant reinforcement of that position is also
important. Put what you need on the table and stay there.
Anchor the position by constantly reinforcing it and not
moving from it. This idea that somehow you should ask for
twice what you need, then haggle, is old hat and can damage

your long-term relationships. What you may need to do is be flexible in other areas to protect the areas where you can't be flexible.

My advice?

Tell them exactly what you want early in the negotiation – especially when what you want is far removed from the status quo.

Anchor yourself at that position and remind the other side constantly.

Be open about where you might be flexible if you have to be; incentivise the other side to give you what you want on the important issues.

High bar of collaboration – Even sports people can see the advantages of collaboration over competition...

Horace McDonald

(Published 21st August 2021)

Much like the rest of the nation, having gorged on Euro 2020 and despite it taking only a day to get over the disappointment of England (inevitably) losing the final to Italy on penalties, I took a brief pause before similarly indulging myself in the Olympics – Tokyo 2020. I don't know about you, but for me, it's all about the athletics. While the time difference made it difficult to watch many of the events live, its consumption was very much helped by access to BBC iPlayer, provided it was possible to avoid the results. It was great to be able to watch key finals at a time that suited me and without having to endure the much wasted time between events when watching live. Some of you may remember the classic episode of *The Likely Lads*, an early-1970s British comedy, where in an episode called 'No Hiding Place' the two main protagonists, played by James Bolam and Rodney Bewes, were challenged in a bet to avoid knowing the score of an England game before the TV highlights that were due to be shown that evening. In the modern world where technology is throwing news at you constantly, it's almost impossible for the element of surprise to remain intact.

Recent years have seen a proliferation of new sports added to the Olympic calendar. While I'm sure BMX and skateboarding are wildly popular, I'm not convinced about them as Olympic sports, but the International Olympics Committee needs to do something to maintain interest in the event, particularly amongst younger age groups, many of whom are being lured away to the US football and basketball leagues as well as virtual sports.

I'm a strong believer that the Olympics should only contain those sports where winning the gold medal is the pinnacle in achievement. So, undeniably yes to athletics, gymnastics and swimming but no to football, tennis and golf! (That said, while not a huge rugby fan, I did marvel at the Rugby Sevens.) Tennis player Sascha Zverev can talk all he likes about winning a gold medal being the pinnacle of the sport, but when he looks back on his career, no one will give a damn, particularly as he's yet to win a Grand Slam event, which is the yardstick of success at the top level in tennis. As a huge Roger Federer fan, I did take delight in Zverev knocking out Novak Djokovic in the semi-final, thus denying the latter the opportunity to win every Grand Slam and the

Olympics in the same year, known as the Golden Slam, which has never been done in the men's game (the wonderful Steffi Graf achieved it in women's tennis in 1988).

Tokyo 2020 will live long in the memory. Despite the absence of spectators, the inevitable Covid protocols and the starting officials seemingly having no idea how to manage the simple process of starting a race (I've seen people at school sports' days do a better job), many of the smaller nations did very well and there were a number of amazing performances. Highlights for me were Sydney McLaughlin and Karsten Warholm smashing the 400m hurdles world records in the women's and men's finals, respectively; the women's 100m final, won by Jamaica's Elaine Thompson-Herah, who achieved her second double of 100m and 200m wins. The lowlight was GB snatching a silver medal from the jaws of the gold medal by being pipped on the line by, you guessed it, the Italian 4x100m relay team!

But the biggest highlight for me was the men's high jump final. Not only was it a classic lasting over two and a half hours, but it also ended in three athletes all achieving the same highest clearances at 2.37m and all three failing in their three attempts at 2.39m. If jumpers achieve the same clearance height, they are then separated by the number of failed attempts, which left two jumpers, the Italian, Gianmarco Tamberi,[18] and Qatari, Mutaz Essa Barshim,[19] tying for the lead as they had identical records in not having failed a height before 2.39m. The expectation at that point is that their

---

[18] www.en.wikipedia.org/wiki/Gianmarco_Tamberi
[19] www.en.wikipedia.org/wiki/Mutaz_Essa_Barshim

competitive instincts would have forced them to compete in a 'jump-off' (analogies to penalty shoot-outs anyone?) to decide who would take home the gold medal, and indeed that is what international rules state on how the competition should have ended. A jump-off starts at the next greater height, each jumper has one attempt, and the bar is lowered until one jumper succeeds over the other at one height.

As the two protagonists huddled briefly with the competition official to discuss the offer of a jump-off, in what can only be described as a piece of negotiation brilliance, Barshim was heard to ask, 'Can we have two golds?' He recognised that collaboration would enable both athletes to win, rather than be subject to a gruelling win-lose mini-competition. Once the official responded, 'I think so', the two celebrated together in a joyous way that I've seldom seen. I've rarely been as emotionally moved in my entire life. It was a fitting end to a fascinating and enthralling competition.

Cash or card – The more specific your proposal, the better...

Romana Henry

(Published 25th February 2021)

The global pandemic has changed, and will continue to change, our world in so many ways.

Don't know about you but I cannot imagine how we will ever go back to indoor cinema visits, concerts and festivals, night clubs (for my kids!), rugby and football matches. I'm sure we will, but I also think everything will be done rather differently, hopefully for the better. Unlike many, I love change!

The annual International Edinburgh Festival was one of many significant events cancelled in 2020 (and then 2021), for the first time since its inception in 1947. Although devastating for all those working in the arts, tourism and hospitality, the upside was that Edinburgh residents were able to enjoy the delights of an unusually empty city in August. The first cancellation will serve as a sad reminder of how devastating the pandemic has been to so many. No one expected that 2021 would also be as good as wiped out by Covid, yet here we were, stuck at home, no festival, no travel, no holidays, no pubs or restaurants, no hugs. It's the only time we wish we were older so we could get bumped up the queue to get the vaccine! We missed the tourists, the buzz, the amazing concerts, plays and events, and the city will miss the additional huge amount of revenue the festival generates. Our kids missed the seasonal jobs that were easy to secure, great experience for them and great fun.

I read that the pandemic has accelerated the use of cards in lieu of cash, and while for some there are clearly upsides, there are downsides to others.

Think of the street performers and buskers who relied on cash donations – apparently some now have their own 'contactless donations' hand-held devices! I am struggling to imagine the thousands of street performers in the Edinburgh Festival getting the public to hang around after a performance, queuing up with their credit cards to make a donation! I'm sure we'll all adjust to whatever solution is presented; I hope so.

That got me thinking about all the beggars I saw from my then permitted daily exercise that I still see as I cycle around the quiet streets of Edinburgh, of which, I am ashamed to say, there are far too many. Have you noticed how very empty their hats are, though, as they ask for spare change – and no one has any cash! No hand-held money collecting devices for them (yet?). How on earth are they surviving with so little cash? Many, I suspect, are not.

An experiment was carried out at a university in the US several years ago, where three groups of students were asked to dress as beggars and go sit around the streets. Each group had a sign displayed asking for varying amounts of money.

Group 1 – 'spare change';

Group 2 – 'a quarter';

Group 3 – ' 37 cents'.

Guess which group got the highest amount of donations? Group 3. Why? Because they asked for a very specific amount which, even though it was more than the 'quarter', which arguably is also specific but more generic in terminology, leading people to assume that because the number was so precise, it must be needed for a particular cause.

This is good advice for negotiators who are often not specific with what they want, need, and can or can't do, and expect the other party to read their minds or guess. Dangerous assumption as very rarely will they guess at your favoured end of the deal and you will have to then do a lot of work to try to drag them to where you want them.

So, in a negotiation don't be afraid to ask for what you want; tell the other side upfront what you can and cannot do. Don't be vague, unless you have a lot of time to waste and like to be disappointed.

Let's be clear – The importance of clarity in communication

Alan Smith

(Published 18th December 2019)

Let's get one thing clear.

I can't get over how confusing it all is, to be honest.

The amount of information being thrown at us daily is literally staggering. Much of it playing around in my head and against much of what I used to think was true, contradictory to other snippets, or even fathomable.

Princes accused of dallying and visiting Pizza Express (can't decide which is most believable, but there is certainly nothing amusing about abuse), the world's richest nation suggesting that climate change is a mistake propagated by all the pre-eminent scientists, ducks being taken to court in France for quacking and keeping people up at night, fishing the oceans dry to make protein to feed to cattle to keep us in burgers, cattle creating enough methane to fry the planet (if you watched *Meat: A threat to our planet* on BBC1 you will know what I mean. Depressing or what!).[20]

What on earth is going on?

Against all this backdrop, do we not all crave a bit of clarity? A simple one-dimensional story that at least we can understand and perhaps believe.

The possibility that critical analysis, empathy and other deep human processes could become the unintended

---

[20] BBC 1 *Meat: A threat to our planet* (first aired 25th November 2019)

'collateral damage' of our information culture is not a simple issue. The subtle breakdown of critical analysis and empathy affects us all. It affects our ability to navigate a constant bombardment of information. It incentivises a retreat to the most familiar silos of unchecked information, which require and receive no analysis, leaving us susceptible to false information and prejudice.

Skimming information becomes the only option when you are bombarded with headlines from hundreds, if not thousands, of news sources.

It's probably the best way to sift through the insane amount of content produced daily.

That for me is the only interesting thing about Boris Johnson's message during this general election in the UK.

His cut-through message is to 'Get Brexit Done'. Simple.

Against the other parties who are presenting far more complex and confusing messages, you can see the attraction (even for a passionate remainer like me). His clarity of message and communication seems to have cut through, and I know it is more complicated than just that, believe me.

For those of us tasked with communication and working with others to deliver a message, it seems that there are two real lessons from the Johnson story.

The first is to be utterly clear about what it is that we want to achieve. Try to boil down the way we communicate that to a simple proposition or proposal, as much as possible. Think sentence rather than novel.

Of course, it might need to be substantiated, but try not to confuse that with the clarity of the proposal itself.

The second is to drive that proposal as hard as you can. Communicated clearly, driven hard, proposals are the things that can move the argument on. There are a few caveats to that of course. But nice to start somewhere.

THE 8-STEPS

CHAPTER 5

PACKAGING TO CREATE MORE VALUE

If your proposal is not acceptable to the other party, it is because it either does not address their needs and excites their inhibitions or because it is simply not enough. If it is the former, then it is a packaging issue; if it is the latter, it is a bargaining issue. If you have opened realistically, then very often it is possible to reach a deal without making any further concessions. In order to do so you must first identify the **inhibitions** and the **interests** and address the package to them. If you adopt a **competitive** stance then it is less likely that you will be told about the inhibitions and interests than if you adopt a **co-operative** stance. *Proposals are solutions to needs*: before you begin to respond to a proposal attempt to identify the need; there may be another solution to the problem which involves a lower cost. *Think creatively about the variables*: the first item on any list of variables is **time**.

It is vitally important to *value your concessions in the other party's terms*: what is it worth to the other party? We distinguish responses to negotiations along these lines that we describe as being 'Sumo' or 'Judo'. In Sumo, when receiving a proposal, there can be a tendency for the receiving party to make their proposal with no consideration to the proposal received; think of it like two Sumo wrestlers going at one another aggressively with their proposals, which, if not contained, move the negotiation back to the **Argue** Step and are counterproductive. Judo, by contrast, is subtler, as it requires each fighter to understand what the other fighter is trying to do, work with it and use it to their advantage.

The right thing – Why sanctions are important

Annabel Shorter

(Published 6th February 2020)

Some time ago the government started a process of decriminalising the non-payment of the BBC's licence fee, while at the same time extending the duty to pay to all households including the previously exempt over-75s.

However, by removing the sanction attached to non-payment, do they effectively make it optional? The question is: what percentage of households, given the choice, would pay the fee?

I heard one expert estimate that it would result in a £350m drop in revenue.

So, were the government labouring under the view that people will do the 'right thing'?

My niece and nephew visited me after school recently. They were horrified as they told me that they had been sent around the school during parents' afternoon to offer home-baked cakes in return for donations for the Macmillan coffee morning campaign.

A 'gentleman' that they knew to be comfortably well-off (and generally not afraid to tell you that!) had asked them:

'How much?'

'Whatever you think,' they replied, and held out the collection box.

Apparently, with great relish, they told me how he took a napkin and theatrically piled it with as many cakes as he could hold and went on to grin at them as he put a 10p coin in the box!

Of course, he is a special breed of (insert expletive) but we must recognise that given the chance to do the 'right thing' many people just won't, and for lots of reasons. People might pay the licence fee for the first year, and maybe the second. But who is to say that by the time they have listened to the same voices bragging that they haven't paid, they won't reconsider?

The moral high ground may eventually lose its lustre.

We tell people to be specific about what they want. In the case of the BBC, £154.50 for a colour licence at the time I write this (worth it for David Attenborough alone?).

But if you have no sanction to apply for non-agreement in a negotiation then it may be no more effective than saying 'whatever you think'!

Loss adjusters – Always get to give...

Tom Feinson

(Published 29th March 2018)

Don't ask me how but I managed to acquire a reader subscription account to the *Financial Times* recently. As a result, I thought I should check it out. To be honest, most of it goes above my head but I did notice an article on the two leaders of the Brexit negotiations, Michel Barnier and David Davies. This seemed more like home territory for me.

One thing that stood out was a quote attributed to David Davies taken from his book, *How to Turn Around a Company*.[21] It goes like this:

Make piecemeal concessions, with a declining concession pattern, and keep all concessions low.

This is quite sophisticated thinking for our friend Davies, something he's not known for.

Attitudes to loss and gain have been investigated by researching the psychology of finding and losing money, and they make interesting reading. We all like to find money, but there are implications to how we find it.

Which of these scenarios would you prefer?

---

[21] D. Davies *How to Turn Around a Company* (1988)

Scenario A:

While walking down the street, you find a £20 note.

Scenario B:

While walking down the street, you find a £10 note. The next day, you find another £10 note.

The total amount of money found is the same in each scenario – yet the vast majority of people report that Scenario B would make them happier.

When you reverse the situation, which scenario would you prefer?

Scenario A:

While walking down the street, you lose a £20 note.

Scenario B:

While walking down the street, you lose a £10 note. The next day, you lose another £10 note.

The inverse happens, we would rather lose £20 in one go than £10 on two separate occasions.

Research (beginning with the work of the late Amos Tversky in the 1970s and continued by Nobel Prize laureate Daniel Kahneman) demonstrates that while most of us prefer to get bad news all at once, we prefer to get good news in instalments.

So, well done Davies, big pat on the back then?!

The only thing you forgot was to get something in return. It doesn't matter how sophisticated or otherwise your concession strategy is; if you don't get something in return you are only ever giving stuff away and that's not a good place to be.

It is sensible to have a concession strategy; all good negotiators know they will have to make concessions, but always make sure you have a demand strategy to match it. Given the above insight, I would make sure my demand strategy was the opposite of my concession strategy.

Taxi! – Managing complexity...

Ann McAleavy

(Published 24th February 2022)

Let me set the scene! It's a Saturday night out, you're heading into town for dinner at the new fashionable eatery, then drinks at your favourite bar, and then if you're still standing you head to a club to dance into the wee small hours. At every stage, you hail a taxi and then on the last stretch you book or hail *the* taxi home!

Over the next few years, taxi businesses that have diesel-powered vehicles are being excluded from entering Glasgow city centre in an attempt to be compliant with the city's environmental policy. As much as I applaud efforts to make the city and world greener for my generation and the ones to follow, the immediate impact on lives is an issue that is happening now.

In Glasgow, the well-known Hackney taxi owners are being put under pressure to renew their vehicle to all-electric, or at the very least a Euro 6 vehicle (a diesel vehicle which meets the emission regulations standards) by 1st June 2023. A factor that might not be well known is that the general demographic of the taxi drivers of Glasgow is over 50 years of age. Therefore, there are several problems when buying a new electric taxi. First, the cost is high, approximately £60,000, making it an expensive purchase for those who are heading towards the twilight of their working life, with no way of retiring early to enjoy the fruits of their labour. Second, the current mileage range while operating in full electric mode is under 60 miles; the vehicle then switches to the petrol engine, which currently does not recharge the battery. As a third point, the infrastructure for charging your vehicle is still in its infancy, as these charge points are not widely available.

As we try to deter these vehicles from being in the city, businesses are being forced to close, therefore; will the new fashionable eatery remain open, and will the late-night club be a viable option in the early hours with no transportation options to get home?

As discussions take place in the coming months and years, what should these drivers have on their **must-have** lists, i.e. what I need is an affordable purchase price, versus their **wish** or **concession** lists, i.e. a 300-mile battery life or a changeover date by June 2023? These drivers have a duty to transport people to a destination, for a fair price and in a vehicle that is compliant, while earning a living and paying all associated costs of their business. It's quite a complicated scenario; how can it be navigated?

Is it possible that as a business movement, cities across the country unite and put a proposal forward to include talks on grants available for new and compliant vehicles, and extend the timescale for the changeover by at least one year, allowing a chance to recover from circumstances brought on by Covid measures. Also, provide better infrastructure and an incentive to bring new, younger drivers to the industry, thereby bringing the demographic down in age for the next generation of drivers and securing a viable business.

All the above makes for one hell of a multilateral negotiation; a negotiation for three or more parties, i.e. taxi owners, city councils and business leaders.[22] I urge everyone to prepare, be realistic, package a proposal and agree on the steps about how to move forward. Enough said, I'm off, where's my taxi!!

Gaining 'friendly' advantage –
Harnessing the power of the collective...

David Bannister

(Published 8th November 2018)

Some years ago, a story broke of a shoplifter who stole a tray of cans of beer from a supermarket. This was no ordinary shoplifter, he looked like the actor David Schwimmer and his CCTV photograph was shown widely in the media. David Schwimmer showed his sense of humour by posting his own photograph on social media showing him clutching a similar looking tray of beers and taking a furtive look at a shop camera.

This reminded me of articles I read some time ago about David Schwimmer's role in negotiating the contracts between himself, his five fellow actors in the hugely successful television series *Friends*, and Warner Brothers. I am sure that you will remember *Friends* as an American sitcom set in New York featuring six actors playing the eponymous friends. When the series began all six actors were paid the

---

[22] www.scotwork.co.uk/solutions/ans/

same salary – according to reports, $22,500 per episode. The series was written and presented in such a way that all six actors were given approximately equal airtime in each episode. Apparently, Warner Brothers felt that this gave them leverage in negotiating contracts with the actors because not one of them had more power than any other as the series could cope with losing any one or even two, of them and still continue. As time went on, David Schwimmer and Jennifer Aniston achieved, through their agents, salaries that were approaching double the salary figures achieved by the other four actors. Speaking in an interview, David Schwimmer told how he thought this was unjust even though his agent was suggesting that he should ask for even more money for the following episodes. Schwimmer suggested to his fellow actors that it would be more effective for them to negotiate as a group than as individuals and that they should indicate to Warner Brothers that failure to agree with all of them together would jeopardise the potential for future episodes of a massively lucrative franchised series. Individually, they might be replaceable; collectively they were not. To achieve this objective, Schwimmer offered to reduce his own salary and persuaded Jennifer Aniston to do the same. The outcome was that in Season 3 of the series all six were paid the same: $75,000 per episode. As time went by and the sixth series was being prepared that salary multiplied by 10 for each actor.

Gradually, the actors in the series felt that they would wish to move on and further their careers elsewhere. Warner Brothers, however, had a series that averaged 24.7 million viewers every week, significantly more than any other show on television. Advertising revenues were lucrative because of the young audience and the producers wanted to continue the series for as long as possible. The outcome was that the six actors, in negotiating their ongoing contracts for the final year of *Friends*, were placed in a powerful position. They used this to negotiate salaries of $1 million each per episode – $22 million for each actor for the year. But they didn't stop there and the series' box set became a streaming phenomenon. Recognising this, the six actors negotiated a deal whereby they would gain in an open-ended way for all networked episodes of the series anywhere in the world – forever. It is said that this still earns each of them $20 million a year.

By strategically reframing the relationship between the actors as a collective bargaining group and Warner Brothers, the actors enhanced their value much more than if they had continued to deal as individuals. They appealed to the interest of the producers who wanted to keep the series going for as long as they could, and also – by having the foresight to readjust the salaries of the highest earners – the sacrifice of a few thousand dollars turned into a benefit of many millions. Moreover, using time to project their negotiating leverage into the future secured those earnings even after they had stopped working to provide them.

I share this with you because it illustrates some important negotiating points about examining your own power, increasing your value and using the fact that collective action can trump self-interest, using that collective value to the greatest effect, being brave enough to accept a short-term 'hit' for long-term advantage and recognising how to future-proof your deals. How very clever!

Not going to – If the deal doesn't work, try an incentive

Alan Smith

(Published 26th November 2020)

It came as a blessed relief when the news broke that not one but three vaccines had been proven to be effective in the fight against Covid. Seems that vaccines are a bit like buses, particularly when there is little else to do but look for them, and the profit motive driving the businesses considering them has created a laser-like focus. Cynical? Me? Not at all. If you want something to happen, just give people a real incentive to drive their behaviour. Altruism fuelled by cash is a pungent mix.

You would have thought that everyone would have agreed. But no. Some people, anti-vaxxers as they are called, are against vaccines in any guise.

Public attitudes towards vaccination can be split broadly into three categories. First, there are people who have been persuaded of the merits of vaccination. In the UK, this group constitutes somewhere between 70% and 90% of the population. Second, there are dogmatic anti-vaxxers. 'These are people on the fringes,' explained Vis Viswanath, Professor of Health Communication in the Department of Social and Behavioral Sciences at Harvard; 'they are not going to change their views.' Between the two groups lies a third, comprising the group of people who are undecided. 'These people have legitimate questions,' said Viswanath. 'They want to do the right thing, but they have doubts. This is where we need to be focusing our attention.'

Anti-vaxxers make up a small but significant group of loud people, who are against all kinds of vaccine, not just for Covid. They persist with a series of arguments for which there is no scientific evidence but that generate hesitancy among an alarming number of people who, due to the success of vaccination itself, have forgotten that not so long ago many were dying from diseases such as diphtheria, polio or measles.

So, what does society do to encourage their interest in taking vaccines, and not allow them to freeload on those that do decide to do the right thing and try to beat this virus? (My views are clearly my own and are not intended to represent those of my colleagues as a whole, but I suspect they do.)

I put these points to my daughter when she was training to be a GP. She said while committed anti-vaxxers display a sort of religious zealotry that makes attempts at dialogue deeply frustrating, there is no reason to dismiss the concerns of people who worry about the vaccines. Putting pressure on people, shaming them or forcing them to do something that they are scared of is not a good idea. Most people are reasonable; give them the data and they are only too pleased that they have access to life-saving vaccinations. Very judicious and persuasive.

I'm not sure. But I do know if you don't have something the other side wants or would rather avoid, getting them to do anything is pretty tough.

Globally, some governments have implemented a number of sanctions against those who decide not to take the vaccine. Not letting them into pubs, gyms or public places, and even denying healthcare and not allowing their children into school, despite the logistical problems intrinsic in setting up health passports.

I'd rather incentivise, but if that doesn't work, what option do you have.

Having your cake, and eating it –
Asking questions to better understand the other party's needs...

Ellis Croft

(Published 18ᵗʰ August 2022)

One of the myriad ways in which our childhood negotiation skills are blunted as we grow up is the life lesson that we're not always going to get what we want. While that's sound advice and true, in negotiation terms it tends to form unnecessary and bad habits when it comes to how we respond to the other party saying 'no' – the tendency to assume it's because we've asked for too much, or offered too little, can become automatic. That means we trade value before, or instead of, exploring alternative possibilities as to why the other party might have turned our proposal down.

I was recently at a friend's significant birthday bash, and it brought to mind a memory of how this manifests itself in the real world. My friend had spent a few years in Australia in the late 1990s, and it being a pre-Zoom world with dial-up internet, had not had the opportunity to secure employment in advance of her move down under. Despite numerous conversations with Australian embassy staff, no solution to this dilemma had arisen, and she had therefore found herself interviewing for full-time work while on a tourist visa – a less than ideal situation. However, her CV was excellent – blue-chip, global companies, a history of achievement and even an award or two – so the interest from potential employers was keen. Offers, however, were drier than a dingo's nose on a hot outback afternoon. My friend was seriously considering whether she ought to dramatically lower her salary expectations in order to change this situation, although she was baffled as the feedback she had been getting was entirely positive. It was the absence of job offers – the rejection of her proposals – that was the problem. We were in touch via email during this period, and I got in touch with an old friend and colleague, who'd ended up in a senior HR position in Melbourne, to explain the situation and see whether any useful insights might be forthcoming. My HR friend explained that the obvious blocker was the visa situation. Potential employers were terrified that my friend – having an exemplary CV, great experience and highly marketable capabilities – would use them to get a change of visa status before moving on to a better paid position elsewhere, leaving them with various liabilities and costs around the need to re-apply for the right visa. Aussies are generally more direct than their British counterparts, but even so, there was a reluctance to share this rather accusatory information with my friend.

I contacted my friend and suggested that she gently probe this objection when the opportunity next came up – and indeed, she was told that 'this has happened before' more than once. So the problem wasn't that she was asking too much – far from it. We quickly realised that the amount in the proposal wasn't the issue, but how it was structured – a packaging question, rather than a bargaining one. My friend came up with a creative solution whereby she proposed that any cost involved in changing visa status would be amortised over her first 18 months of employment, and if she left for any reason before the end of that period, she would owe the employer the balance remaining. For her, this concession was easy (she knew the probability of leaving for any reason was slim as she had done her research on the potential employers), but crucially she valued it based on the employer's perspective. Within a week of repackaging her proposals to employers, she had three strong offers, and even took a call from the Chief Financial Officer of one to say how pleased they were to be able to offer a key role to somebody who clearly understood negotiation so well (a smart move – she spent a number of successful years with that employer).

'Cakeism' can be seen as a generally derogatory term, denoting entitlement and privilege – but to a skilled negotiator, it's a habit to establish whether the cake simply needs to be sliced differently before assuming that it's the size of the cake that's the obstacle.

Get your kicks from future–proofed deals – it's all a matter of goals! – The future isn't certain, but it can be planned for...

David Bannister

(Published 17th February 2016)

I read an interesting article based on the work of a renowned US business school, which gave the results of studies into mergers and acquisitions in international business over a period of years. The conclusion, briefly summarised, was that what these deals produced in practice was a long way short of what had been predicted for them at the outset – fewer than a third of deals met the expectations that had been heralded for them when they were being contemplated and shareholders were being convinced to endorse them. It is interesting that some of Scotwork's emerging research into negotiating behaviours (we will be saying more about this in the months to come) indicates that untrained negotiators don't see the negotiating process as adding a great deal of long-term business value or as strengthening relationships. It seems the process is just a necessary evil to many who have to carry it out. Trained negotiators, however, seem to have a different view.

I was put in mind of these things when I read a brief article recently in the *Times* newspaper. It concerned a deal done between two football clubs: Monaco and Manchester United (I declare an interest here, I am a passionate and very long-term supporter of the latter team). The deal concerned a young player, Anthony Martial, who was transferred to Manchester United from Monaco in 2015. The deal, for a reported fee of €80 million, was the largest ever for a teenage footballer – Martial was 19 years old at the time. Other details of the deal have, however, been leaked and include some interesting features. If Martial scores 25 goals in competitive matches for Manchester United, Monaco will be entitled to a payment of €10 million. Moreover, if he is shortlisted for the Ballon d'Or (the soccer equivalent of the Oscars) then a further €10 million is due to Monaco. If, however, Martial achieves neither of these desirable targets then Manchester United could sell the player, but if he is sold before 2018 for a figure between €60 million and €100 million, then Monaco will earn 50% of the profit that Manchester United make.

This intrigued me; how clever were the Monaco negotiators to recognise the importance of such a player to the Manchester club and to future-proof the deal when they recognised that they would not be able to keep their young asset for themselves? All negotiated deals necessarily involve an element of risk – we change the status quo in the belief at the time that we will benefit from the negotiated change. However, it may be a good lesson for us all to learn from the Monegasque negotiators that the deal we do can include a component to minimise the risk associated with the deal. Of course, none of us know the compromises that took place to get the deal through at the €80 million price in the first place, but thinking creatively about how many elements you can include in your deals and recognising that you can trade against future events and benefit from them is genuinely creative.

Me? I just wish Anthony Martial was scoring only just enough goals to put that €10 million payment in danger!

Car trouble – Packaging for success...

Horace McDonald

(Published 14th April 2022)

On a recent car journey from London to Shropshire, I received a message from an old friend asking if I had time for him to pick my brain (fortunately for him, my wife was driving – she has the stamina of a long-distance lorry driver).

As I get older these requests are becoming more frequent, as I have two areas of expertise, of which negotiation is one (the other one is an ability to recite a list of professional footballers who have first-class degrees, but I don't get many calls asking for that).

My friend runs a specialist online marketplace that offers a broad range of products, within a high-profile niche. The business is going through the familiar growing pains of navigating funding rounds, investors who always want more and unpredictable demand. He called as, despite being under contract, his biggest supplier wanted improved commercial terms. It was clear that the supplier partner was in a position of some power: it accounted for a significant proportion of my friend's business, and it had other channels to market.

Humans are competitive; it is not uncommon for people in these sorts of situations to want to take an aggressive position and not negotiate. At Scotwork we recognise that negotiation is only one of the options available to resolve conflict, and it was clear that while this option was available to the supplier partner it was not viable for my friend's business.

The conversation was not dissimilar to one we'd had many years ago when he found himself in conflict with a business partner. I advised him to take a value-enhancing solution rather than a competitive one, which was the advice he was getting from everyone else he'd spoken to. The situation was successfully resolved and he often mentions it when I see him. Despite this, his ego got the better of him this time and he wanted to fight, based on the contractual situation. You won't be surprised to hear that my advice was that while this might satisfy his ego, it would likely be damaging in the longer term.

In these situations, both preparation and creativity come to the fore in negotiation. My advice was to create a **wish list** of the things his business would need in order to be able to meet some or all of the supplier's demands. If the extent of the demand is unpalatable then the requirements needed to meet it need to be equally so. In complex negotiation scenarios, the demands of both parties typically span different variables; however, this was not the case here. I advised him to link the different areas in his **wish list** item to staged increases in margin. In this instance, there is a danger in offering a proposal that gives them everything they need in return for everything you need, as they tend to become fixated on your ability to meet their demand and less interested in the concessions required to achieve them.

The deal was concluded in a satisfactory manner. As in every negotiation, my friend had to give some things up but kept a very important supplier, and thankfully well before my wife had stopped driving.

Me, myself and I! – The power of good advice...

Alan Smith

(Published 4th July 2019)

Great negotiators are judiciously self-aware. They understand how they are being impacted by a negotiation, why they are feeling threatened or how they are preening at the expense of the other side(s). This enables them to keep their focus on what is most important – the outputs they need. Being critically self-aware is often a basis for making sure their characters are put in check.

Many years ago, when I ran my own business, I was approached by an organisation who wanted to buy my company. I was both excited about the prospect of realising the equity I had built up over the preceding 12 years, but also keen to be recognised for creating a new brand and business in a difficult trading environment.

When the original offer was made (yes dear reader they drove the process, which I came to recognise was not the best strategy, and thereby structured my expectations over what would and would not be acceptable) my partner and I became outraged. Had they no idea how hard we had worked to build the business, attain our blue-chip clients, employ and retain high calibre staff – what on earth did these bean counters know about the real world! We felt almost personally affronted. Our egos dented.

We took advice from a broker (who frankly had much more mergers and acquisitions negotiation experience than we did) who gave us some sage advice, which I share with you here.

He first asked about how well the business was performing and what the next few years would look like.

We said pretty well, we had been growing significantly and saw that trend continuing. He said now is a good time to sell. He told us that the value that anyone would pay would be based on a multiple of profit over the next three years.

What would you have said, we asked him, if we had said the future was looking rocky? He said his advice would have been the same. Sell now. Why, we asked? He said because if the future was going badly at least we could realise some equity now.

He made us realise that the issue that was driving us was understanding our own objectives and the flexibility we had within these factors (what I would describe as our **intend** and **must** positions).

His advice was to craft a deal that recognised the value we had created, but critically placed a bet against our ambitions for future performance.

Being well prepared by addressing our own realistic objectives gave us the ability to drop our egos out of the discussion and eventually reach a deal that rewarded our performance to that point, and satisfied our ambitions based on the future we could create.

Of course, ego has a place in negotiations. But it shouldn't be the driver.

Embrace your inner flamingo – The dangers of meeting the wrong needs...

David Bannister

(Published 7ᵗʰ October 2021)

Like many of us, I am a frequent online purchaser, and in these difficult times my use of internet shopping has increased. I don't particularly enjoy shops and, where I can, I like the idea of stabbing the keys on my keyboard, ticking the PayPal box or confirming my details with Amazon, and waiting for the doorbell to ring heralding the arrival of my purchases.

There is, I have discovered, a downside to all of this. While buying, all of us give information about ourselves, our contact details and our bank to the sellers. Not only that but the sellers are always busy compiling data on you, your purchases and your apparent retail preferences. When we buy or even enquire about a possible purchase, the potential retailer harvests our information and uses it to try to tempt us with similar goodies at a later time. But recently I have noticed a new, unsolicited annoyance. Having searched the website of one large retailer of household goods for some pillows and another for some outdoor clothing in which they specialise, I received emails from both. One was headed, 'Your final chance to get your pink flamingo' and the other offered me a rather tacky holdall in return for an order above a certain sum. The flamingo offer, on investigation (couldn't help myself – better judgement jettisoned and replaced with overwhelming curiosity), turned out to be a large inflatable pink flamingo of the sort you might, if good taste were not important to you, take to a swimming pool. Honestly, I am not making this up! What you had to do was order a piece of furniture or other household item and your new sofa would arrive together with said blow-up bird. If I had bought, say, a waterproof coat from the other retailer, I would have been given a small, cheap, plastic holdall with the retailer's name prominently displayed so that any foray out with the bag would have me as a walking advertisement for the trader. No thanks on both counts.

Nevertheless, these offers got me thinking about negotiating and value. I have never in my life felt the need for
an inflatable flamingo and I rather take pride in owning nice
luggage so I could see no appeal in the holdall either. Why
then did these purveyors of relatively expensive items think
that the offer of cheap, tacky giveaways would encourage me
or people like me to buy from them? I suppose that they must
place a value on their freebies and so assume that we would
be so grateful to have such an object that we, their customers,
would be persuaded to buy now instead of later. Or perhaps
buy from them instead of a competitor. In reality, I know that
I should have made contact with them both and said, 'Thanks
for the opportunity, but if you are going to offer me a reward
for buying from you, I would prefer pillowcases to go with
my pillows or a pair of socks to go with my waterproof jacket'.
I am not sure if I would have received a reply. Alternatively,
I could have bought the pillowcases and the jacket and kept
the free items but not used them (as I have said, I have no
use for either). Then when I next ordered from them, I could
have said, 'I have here a fine and unused flamingo/holdall and
would be willing to send it back to you if you can let me have
along with my new purchase a pillowcase (or some socks)'.

Now, I hear you say, Bannister has lost his marbles. No
one would fall for that. But they can and they do. In a negotiation, you may get offered a concession you neither anticipate nor want. The message is don't ignore it and certainly
don't reject it; whoever is offering it attaches a value to it –
can you enrich your position by exchanging it for something
you do value or by accepting it to trade back at a later stage or

even on another day? Everything offered has a value, which may not be the same for you as it is for them; try an exchange for something you might value more. I think I am going to call it the 'Inflatable Flamingo Gambit' and include it in the Scotwork course notes!

My final piece of news is that the clothing seller, presumably having unloaded all their logo-stamped holdalls on an unsuspecting clientele, are now offering two coffee mugs decorated with William Morris patterns if you buy from them. Where do they get this stuff??

Play nice! – Packaging for power and control...

Alan Smith

(Published 24th November 2016)

Two questions:

1. When negotiating, do you want the other side to act reasonably?; and
2. Is it a good strategy to be reasonable when negotiating?

Most people will say 'yes' to the first question. It would be crazy not to.

The second, however, creates a bit more of a dilemma. We are sometimes tempted to go high or low, pad and exaggerate what we really anticipate being able to achieve. Because that is what we should do, right?

The problem with going extremely high or low, being unreasonable, is that it encourages the other side to do the same. You start high, they go low, the dance begins, the handbags are placed on the dance floor before you eventually converge on a deal that is 'reasonable'. In the meantime, you have both spent a lot of time, energy and money, and potentially done a lot of harm to what could have been a harmonious relationship.

Would it be to everyone's advantage to come to the table with a realistic starting position? Not soft, certainly challenging and ambitious, but with a foothold in reality, one that can be explained and have its basis understood.

An interesting proposition indeed and one that recently inspired a final-offer negotiation challenge by AIG, an insurance giant. Like many insurance firms they spend billions of pounds across thousands of cases and often end up in court battles dealing with inefficient settlements. Expensive, right?

Also, like many insurance companies they build their reputation on trust and fairness. That is why people use them in the first instance. They certainly do not want to overpay on claims – commercial suicide – but they do need their customers to recognise that they want to do the right thing.

AIG created a final-offer arbitration mechanism to try to speed up dealing with claims. Essentially, parties on either side of the claim would make an offer and present them to an arbitrator who would then decide which offer was most fair. That would be the legally binding offer going forward. No splitting the difference or further negotiation.

AIG took the view that if they made an offer that was reasonable and the other side didn't, their offer would be the one that carried the day. They also opined that this would be seen as fair to their important customers and that it would encourage them to come to the table with a reasonable offer in return. Fairness was actually built into the system.

Apparently, the system has shown some degree of success.

The challenge for such a methodology in the commercial world is of course who decides what is fair? What margin should your bid be allowed to have built in? How many migrants should be allowed across your borders to protect free trade? What time should you be able to come home if you tidy your room?

Fairness may just be in the eye of the beholder.

Currying favour – How not understanding your customer damages your business...

Horace McDonald

(Published 17th March 2022)

Some weeks ago, I went out with a very old friend (we were best man at each other's weddings). Despite both growing up in south-east London, we now live in west London, pretty close to one another. My friend's heritage is a mix of Asian-Trinidadian and Irish and, perhaps unsurprisingly, our evening comprised a couple of beers (I prefer Guinness and he Peroni) in a local Irish pub, followed by a meal at a local Indian restaurant. I have to admit to being a little bit in awe of him when we go out for Indian food, as I marvel at his ability to substitute chapattis for a knife and fork.

The restaurant we visited has a long history in the area and is situated in a fairly affluent part of west London. On this particular Saturday evening, the restaurant was about one-third full, as we'd just recently emerged from the worst of the pandemic, which was clearly still restricting people's appetite for eating out. When ordering our meal, we entered into a conversation with the waiter/proprietor about their pricing, as he had commented that despite significant increases in raw material costs they had not been able to increase their prices for a number of years.

This viewpoint struck me as a little bit odd and I gently tried to open up the conversation to explore what was stopping them from reviewing their pricing strategy. As mentioned earlier, the restaurant is situated in a pretty well-heeled area, and there are a number of restaurants in close proximity, but no Indian restaurants; the close proximity of three or four decent pubs in the area is also a benefit. What struck me was that the proprietor was looking at the situation from their own perspective rather than taking a broader view of how his clientele operated.

Unlike most restaurants, Indian restaurants tend not to display their menus in the windows and, even if they do, most people rarely look at them. People tend to know what they like and it's more about mood. In my experience of observing people in these restaurants, people typically walk straight in without much deliberation, are then seated and the first thing they do is order a drink (usually alcoholic) and poppadoms. My sense is that while people have an understanding of what their favourite meal costs, within certain parameters, the likelihood that a customer would end up walking out of the restaurant because the price of their favourite dish had increased by 10% is negligible and the vast majority of them wouldn't even notice.

I tried to mention some of these factors in the conversation but it fell on deaf ears. It struck me that he was almost gripped by fear at the prospect of putting his prices up. In any negotiation there are unknowns; expert negotiators are aware of this and use whatever means necessary to get as much information about the other party's position as possible. They do this by gathering information through desk research and preparing the appropriate questions in advance to ensure that they elicit the information they need. They are mindful that making assumptions is dangerous and wherever possible they use the negotiation process to test assumptions through asking questions and summarising the other party's position.[23] Indeed, the restaurant could easily have tested different price points to challenge their assumptions.

My view is that this restaurant is losing money through fear of putting up its prices and a lack of understanding of how its customers think: not a good place for a business owner or negotiator to be in.

Be a negotiator – tickle the ivories! – Repackaging to create value...

David Bannister

(Published 15th April 2021)

A letter to the *Times* newspaper told of a man who no longer wanted a piano he owned. He put it on the driveway to his house with a sign on it indicating it would be available free to

---

[23] www.scotwork.co.uk/solutions/ans/

a good home. No takers. So he changed the sign to say 'piano for sale - £100'. It was stolen overnight.

The story reminded me of an experience of my own when I was consulting to a large international law firm. A senior partner told me that he and colleagues offered free client seminars on relevant topics on which they were expert. He lamented the fact that, despite booking on the seminars, many clients cancelled at short notice or did not turn up and did so often without apology. Try charging them, I suggested. His response was that my suggestion did not make any sense – if they would not come to a free seminar, they clearly would not come if they were charged. I persisted and he said he would consider the change (more to prove me wrong than because he believed me, I suspect). A few months later he sought me out when I was at his office to say that both take up and attendance at the seminars had increased despite the charge. Not only that but clients stayed for lunch and more useful contact was made. 'Why?' he asked. I suggested that the clients perhaps thought that they might miss something valuable because the price somehow quantified a value. Human psychology is a funny thing, but I am sure that was the reason.

The issue of value and how we create it is an important one for all of us who negotiate. We know from our extensive studies that giving things away during a negotiation not only elicits indifference (as with the piano), it even engenders greed – 'give me more!'. Like my lawyer client, the more we work to show the value of what we have to offer to those we negotiate with, the more we provide ourselves with the capital for our negotiated deals. Also, like my lawyer client, this is increasingly true when we are under pressure. Scotwork's Negotiating Capability Survey shows us that the more unskilled negotiators feel that the other party has an advantage, the more likely they are to offer them the negotiator's equivalent of a free piano and the less likely the other party is to be impressed by it.[24] Remember to explore value to the other party, emphasise and exploit it by asking for something in return, for anything you offer equivalent to the value the offer represents to the other party – even if, really, it's something *you* no longer place great value in. To be a negotiator, think piano!

A van story – The importance of 'know what you want and how you can get it' when you have a complaint...

Horace McDonald

(Published 28th April 2021)

Much has been written about how the lockdown has impacted younger people both in terms of work opportunities and the lack of engagement with colleagues to develop the key work relationships so vital in the early stages of their careers. Covid also exerted huge pressure on social relationships, particularly those of younger people who are in new relationships, or those who have only recently started cohabiting. A good friend of mine told me a story about how his son and (newish) partner had recently moved into a flat in London, and that unexpected strains started appearing as they were

---

[24] www.scotwork.com/solutions/capability-survey/

spending all day together in a very nice but rather small flat. This situation is not uncommon as these dwellings are not built on the basis that both occupants will be in there 24/7. We all need our space, don't we?

The pandemic has also resulted in some couples cohabiting earlier than they would otherwise have planned. I have a good friend, twice divorced, for whom this has been a blessing as he's moved in with his partner and her teenage daughters and things are going very well. Less fortunate was a close family member (let's call that person FM) and it was a very difficult time. The break-up resulted in FM coming to live with my wife and me and our two adult children. Early on we needed to organise moving FM out of the apartment shared with the partner. I hired a van from one of the national hire companies, which I'd used previously on a number of occasions. The day of the move was very emotional and my wife managed that side of things (she's just better at it than me) and I did mostly (non-emotional) heavy lifting. Having made many trips up and down the stairs carrying large boxes and various paraphernalia, by late afternoon we had finally emptied the flat. And would you believe it, the van wouldn't start!

Some three hours and two separate visits later, from Mercedes-Benz and the AA, we finally got the van going again. During the intensive analysis by the AA van, I spotted that the battery was from a different car manufacturer, and the lovely AA guy and I deduced that someone had hired the van to swap out the battery (and no doubt had also claimed a refund when it went wrong). On the first call with the breakdown service, we also discovered that the van had experienced the same problem during its last hire. Strangely, this rather calamitous series of episodes resulted in the three of us having quite a laugh about the whole thing despite the rather trying circumstances. I suppose it's better to laugh than cry. The following morning, when we'd hoped to deposit the contents of the van into the storage locker we'd hired, yes, you guessed it, the van wouldn't start again. The hire company had to send a pickup truck for the broken-down van and we had to move all of the stuff in that van into a new van which they delivered to us.

By day two I'd gone through the denial phase (this can't be happening) and the acceptance phase (it is and I can't change it) and started thinking about what remedies I could extract from the hire company. Getting the money back for the cost of the hire was the easy bit; the next thing to think about was how I could get them to compensate me for the aggravation suffered. The first thought that comes to most people's minds is about money and no doubt it would have been possible to have got some money out of them, but how does one really quantify this given all the above took place over Bank Holiday weekend and they could argue this had already been compensated for by the refund of the hire? I also realised that it was likely that the local shop itself had limited options beyond the refund. As a negotiator, the thought then turned to value: what could I get from them that had relatively low cost to them but high value to me? In this way I would be able to get more than they could give me in cold hard cash. The next thought was about who would be empowered to make the higher-level decision. The fault wasn't deliberate on the hire firm's part, but what was clear was that the knowledge about the earlier breakdown meant that their process wasn't working well. This enabled me to get to the Area Manager and secure two free additional hires that I need to transport my son's gear to get him to and from university before he completes his studies, which has saved me a considerable sum.

THE 8-STEPS

CHAPTER 6

BARGAIN TO CREATE MORE VALUE

At Scotwork, we passionately believe that any proposal you make should be one that you think the other party can accept. In making one, you should always be ready for a counterproposal, which is when the bargaining process typically starts. However, bargaining can take place at any stage of the negotiation; for information, for concessions, for signals, for time and for the deal itself (see **Close** Step). In the **Proposal** stage of the book, we have covered the disadvantages of making extreme proposals.

Bargaining takes place in a repositioning of variables and is underpinned by one of the most important principles in negotiation – ensure that you get something in return for any concession you make and by valuing your concessions in the other party's terms. Doing so ensures that the value created is maintained by (where possible) trading low-cost items (concessions) for items of high value. Hence, if they ask for more of something, you need to make a proposal that ensures you get (more) value back in return.

How you articulate any bargaining proposal is critical, in that you state the condition before the offer, so by way of example, at the end of dinner with one of your children, rather than say:

'I will let you have ice cream as long as you eat your cabbage.'

It is better to say:

'If (and only if) you eat all your cabbage, then (and only then) will I let you have some ice cream.'

The latter makes a statement, avoids interruption and forces the other party to think of it as a trade- off.

The power of 'no' – The dangers of being too greedy...

Stephen White

(Published 14th May 2015)

The Argentinian film, *Wild Tales*, is a compilation of six unrelated fictions about people in desperate situations.[25] I would recommend it to anyone who likes entertaining storytelling, but one of the segments has particular interest for negotiators.

---

[25] Warner Bros. Pictures *Wild Tales* (2014)

The plot revolves around the wealthy father of a wayward teenager. This teenager takes the family's BMW out for the night, gets drunk and collides with a pregnant pedestrian in a hit-and-run incident. Mother and unborn child don't survive. The teenager confesses to his parents, and the father together with the family lawyer hatches a plan. The gardener, a retainer of many years' standing, is invited to take the rap by claiming to be the driver and serving the prison sentence (expected to be an unrealistic 18 months) in return for $500,000, a sum beyond his dreams.

The father is desperate to keep his son out of prison, and this weakness is exploited as the parties begin to rack up the price. A million-dollar bribe for the policeman who spots inconsistencies in the gardener's story, half a million more for the family's lawyer as a brokerage fee. Then the gardener demands a seaside apartment in addition to his pay-off, and the policeman wants some expenses on top of his. The apartment and the expenses are obvious wish-list items.

But the worm turns. At this last request, the frustrated father says 'no' to the whole deal, withdraws all the offers and says he would rather let his son go to prison. His wife pleads, the lawyer threatens, but to no avail.

With one word the father has switched the balance of power in the negotiation. The lawyer comes back, offering to withdraw the wish-list demands. The father dismisses this and proposes that the whole deal cost him no more than $1 million, shared between the parties as agreed amongst themselves. The lawyer pleads for more money, the father refuses, and the deal is done on the father's terms. There are at least two lessons from this story: first, negotiators should learn how power can shift by their own actions – it is not a fixed given – and second, don't get greedy!

If you are cursing me for spoiling the movie for you, I promise that there is a twist at the end of this segment, and also that the other five stories are also brilliantly entertaining.

Incidentally, the storyline has echoes of the 2008 Turkish movie *Three Monkeys*, which is also well worth watching.[26]

Enjoy.

A fine line – Beware of exercising too much power in your dealmaking; circumstances change...

John McMillan

(Published 1st October 2015)

Two stories in the British press read that oil field services provider, Halliburton, had made an offer to swallow rival Baker Hughes for $35 billion, and that Schlumberger had weighed in on equipment maker Cameron International in a $14.8 billion deal. Companies that specialise in one part of the services market, for example offshore drilling, are in a difficult situation and are finding themselves squeezed by their customers to such an extent that, in order to survive, they are having to accept takeover deals from bigger rivals or risk going out of business; takeover deals that would not have been countenanced 18 months ago are suddenly now acceptable – even welcome!

---

[26] Zeitgeist Films/Pyramide International *Three Monkeys* (2008)

In such a cut-throat environment, the service providers find themselves giving heavy discounts for the few deals that they can secure because customers find themselves with the upper hand at the negotiating table.

North Sea oil producer Enquest, which hires services firms for projects on a regular basis, said it had negotiated discounts of up to 50% on some contracts. The industry consensus on new rates is around 20% below previous years. Enquest's CEO, Amjad Bseisu, told Reuters, 'We give all our contractors notice that we're going to fire them. We sit with them and say, "do you want to negotiate or do you want to bid things out?"'

Because of their weak bargaining position, the services companies also have to take on a higher share of project risks that oil producers are increasingly unwilling to shoulder themselves.

'We are able to be selective, and in different circumstances, to transfer a bit of risk to the service side,' said Tony Durrant, CEO of North Sea oil producer Premier Oil. Rig providers, for example, now charge lower rates for days when their equipment is not used due to poor weather, something that was countenanced a year ago when the risk always lay with the client.

'When rigs are very short, they are quite happy to use their negotiating power. It's a balance,' said Durrant.

All of which goes to demonstrate how the power balance shifts depending on cyclical shifts in the market. Negotiators need to be flexible and to recognise when they have the upper hand (less need for flexibility) or the opposite (more need for flexibility). When the power balance is against you, you need to be very careful not to set unfortunate precedents, but when it is with you, you need to give the other side some room to breathe, so that when their good times come back and the balance shifts back again, they do not want to punish you!

A fine line indeed!

A right royal deal? – If you overestimate your power, you can expect this to be reflected by the counterparty's response...

David Bannister

(Published 23rd January 2020)

For some time, the press in the UK and in other parts of the world has devoted many of its precious column inches to the story surrounding Prince Harry, Duke of Sussex, and his wife, the former actress, Meghan Markle. As you can probably imagine with my background, whenever the word 'negotiation' appears in the press then my attention is caught. In this case, a week or so of discussions and negotiations have taken place between the Prince and members of the British Royal Family. I have found it interesting to reflect on how these negotiations have been reported and I thought I might subject them to some scrutiny. Let me examine here the Royal Family negotiations from a Scotwork perspective.

First, we always tell people to have very clear objectives and to have those prioritised. This particular saga began with an apparently 'out of the blue' statement from the Sussexes to the effect that they wanted to 'step back' from their roles as senior members of the Royal Family, but they would 'honour their duty' to the Queen with whom they would 'collaborate'. Many thought that the statement carried all the hallmarks associated with a PR adviser. For me, the essential question is how realistic were their initial objectives? Stepping back from royal responsibilities but still honouring your duty and collaborating appears to indicate that the terms under which they are prepared to continue as members of the Royal Family would be determined by them and effectively make them part-time members. It has rapidly become evident, if we did not already suspect it, that those born into the Royal Family inherit with that birth a duty to the country and its people. Our then 93-year-old Queen made it clear within days that the stated objective was not going to be achievable, that a 'pick and mix' membership of the Royal Family was not going to be an option and, moreover, that as monarch, no one 'collaborates' with her. The negotiating lesson here, it seems to me, is when you select your objectives to put yourself in the other party's shoes, listen to yourself carefully and assess the realism of your proposal from their standpoint. On this test, the Sussexes' self-centred objectives fell at the first hurdle.

Second, I began to think about power. Many warm words were said in royal statements acknowledging that the desire of the Prince and his wife to live a different life, predominantly in a different country, was something with which the Royals empathised. However, there was a price to be paid – no royal titles, no selective appearances as members of the Royal Family, no more military patronages and I suspect, behind the scenes, a very clear message about their behaviour as independent individuals. The reality here, I think, is that the Sussexes or their advisers sadly misjudged the way in which the Royal Family would exercise its power over them. Effectively, they were told you may have your relocation and your new life. Here is the price you will pay. Take it or leave it. The Royal Family is rarely called upon to flex its muscles but, in this case, its members knew that for its own survival it would have to exercise its decision-making power ruthlessly. Misjudging the power balance in the negotiation can leave the one who does the misjudging damaged as a result.

The third thing I reflected on was the issue of tradeable items – you can only do a deal if you have something the other side wants and they're prepared to trade with you to get it. In this case, in my judgement, it was the Sussexes who were doing the wanting and who were probably advised that their position in the Royal Family and their, albeit waning, personal popularity gave them some leverage. They were quickly disabused of that and I suspect it was made clear that if their financial independence was going to rest on opportunities like voice-overs for Disney then they would not be doing that as their Royal Highnesses. Always check when you negotiate that you have something to trade with – especially where the counterparty has the balance of power in their favour, as was the case here.

One of the other things we talk about to those we coach, train and advise is the use of time as a negotiating variable. It is particularly interesting in this case that a review period of a year has been built into the publicised deal with the Sussexes. Some think that this may give them a way back if their venture does not prove to be a success. Others, me amongst them, think that this is another means of applying pressure, indicating that financial support will be withdrawn by the Prince's father at the end of the period to provide focus and ensure that the deal is implemented fully. Time manifests itself in a number of different ways in negotiations but in this instance, and because it has been used so publicly, I think it was used to apply pressure to obtain compliance with the deal, and perhaps to give some leverage over future behaviour.

Finally, emotion. The Sussexes have had bad press in the UK whether you judge them to deserve it or not. Emotion is often used to bolster and support an argument – especially after the facts have failed to do so. In this case, according to surveys, the general public was not with the Sussexes in their stated desire to keep one foot in the royal camp and one in Netflix. Implementing negotiated decisions is always likely to be easier when they are supported by the general mood of the people around the decision. In this case, rightly or wrongly, while people understood the desire that the Prince and his wife had to change their lives, people also understood that this had to be done under terms which would have the least damaging consequences for the continuity of the British Royal Family. In the end, all deals that are agreed have to be implemented. Our surveys of negotiators indicate that many are often not happy with the lasting effects of their deals. Deals are frequently made by people who do not have the responsibility for implementing them and so the appetite for implementation diminishes as the deal is passed on from the negotiators to the implementers. In this case, the wish on the part of commentators and the public to see a certain kind of 'just' outcome appeared to disadvantage the Sussexes from the outset. The result was a tough deal that caused one British newspaper to describe the Prince as the 'loser'. It seems to me that the lesson is that if there is support for toughness because it is considered to be appropriate, then that toughness is likely to win the day.

All this, of course, was speculation. The Royal Family have been more open than usual in their thinking about this solution but none of us can ever know exactly what went on in the private meetings that have taken place. Nevertheless, we now have an outcome achieved commendably and quickly, as was the wish of the Queen, who seems to have dictated the terms.

Same-page negotiations – Managing complex bargaining situations...

Robin Copland

(Published 1st February 2018)

Most negotiations are more complex than they appear. Even although, on the face of it, party A, the seller (as an example) is meeting party B (the buyer) in a simple transactional negotiation in which, hopefully, differences can be ironed out and traded away so that a deal is done, the truth of the matter is that it is much more complicated than that.

The seller has a constituency that they have to worry about and questions that they have to be able to answer internally.

- Did I get enough in return for any movement from my opening position?;
- Does the deal contribute to the achievement of my personal objectives?;
- Does the deal help my business achieve its overall business targets?;

- Can the commitments I have promised (delivery schedules, marketing support and the like) be honoured in the fulfilment of the agreement?

And then for the buyer, they are often buying on behalf of internal customers with their own needs, aspirations and requirements. Does the deal work not only from their own personal perspective but from the wider angle of the other stakeholders as well?

Even though there are these extra layers of complexity, those kinds of deals remain at the simpler end of the negotiating spectrum. What about the scenario when there are more than two people taking part in the negotiation? What about, for example, the Northern Ireland peace talks that eventually led to the Good Friday agreement? There you had different political parties in the UK, in Ireland and then, just to complicate matters further, in Northern Ireland. Add to that mix various other 'interested' parties ranging from business groupings to paramilitary organisations, the political wings of said paramilitary organisations, organised religions (the Roman Catholic church might have been construed as having an all-Ireland affiliation because of its close links with the country of Ireland, while the various Protestant churches were more pro-unionist) and three independent mediators, one each appointed by Ireland and the UK and a third appointed by the then president of the US, Bill Clinton.

In these tortuous negotiations, there were the head-to-head headline meetings between the leaders, but then there were also informal meetings between the broad coalitions on either side where deals were done and details thrashed out. 'If you, party

A, keep quiet about issue b (a complete embarrassment to most on our side, but which is nonetheless important to party A), and if we get an agreement that covers issues c, d and e, then we will ensure that your voice is heard on issues f, g and h'.

Why were all these meetings and side agreements so necessary? There is nothing that can damage a negotiation more than one of your allies 'going rogue'. It's like a hostage negotiation reaching a crucial point where deals can be done and the lives of innocents saved. Just at the crucial time, some junior tank commander decides to drive their tank onto the lawn to 'show everyone who's the boss' and the whole deal comes tumbling down.

Discipline is the key. In complicated negotiations, everyone on your team needs to be reading from the same script. That means no blurting of personal opinions; no raising of past transgressions/conflict; no barbed comments; no press briefings by 'sources close to the negotiating team'.

In short, these negotiations need to be conducted from the same page in a disciplined manner. The great dealmaker himself might want to learn a hard-earned lesson or two from those who perhaps know better.

Let's go fly a kite – The benefits of an effective counterproposal

Ellis Croft

(Published 7th April 2022)

My young daughter loves the original *Mary Poppins* film, which is great because it's a fondly remembered slice of my childhood as well. My favourite part of the film is the final song, 'Let's Go Fly a Kite', which ties together both story and the more complex narrative around familial relationships, with a rousing melody to boot. Kite flying is also – as commercial readers will be fully aware – a slightly cheeky tactic some negotiators will use to improve their end of the deal. It usually comes into play late on, as the deal nears a close. Sometimes it goes beyond cheeky and into the realms of the unreasonable demand, of course.

Before Christmas, I was catching up with an old friend who was buying a property in Scotland and wanted to share a problem that had arisen. The vendor, having verbally agreed to the offer my friend had put in for the property, had got in touch to suggest that the deal needed to include an additional £2,000 to allow the property's existing furniture to be included in the sale price. My friend and I had attended a Scotwork course (back in the day; not quite Dick van Dyke's time, but long enough ago) and as a result he'd been diligent and robust in his preparation to negotiate the property deal.[27] The additional £2,000 was within his financial limit, but he saw the demand as an irritant and, as such, not a reasonable one to address with being flexible on the purchase price. He understood that trying to argue the demand off the table (the furniture was barely worth £2,000 when it was new; he had his own furniture to move in, and so on) would be a waste of time and lead to further spurious demands. What he wanted to discuss were alternatives to simply saying 'no' – he was convinced that the vendor was, in his words, 'at it' and that a rebuttal would simply produce an alternative demand for

---

[27] www.scotwork.co.uk/solutions/ans/

additional cost be it based on fittings, light bulbs or anything else that popped into the vendor's imagination. He was, in my friend's view, kite flying.

One of the techniques we were recommended is to put a price on the other party's demands – specifically, where that demand is unreasonable, one that mirrors it. Rather than simply refusing and saying 'no' (which leaves the other party with the initiative, enabling them to come back with another proposal), putting an unrealistic price on an unreasonable demand can effectively block the other party's use of the tactic. Furthermore, it should enable you to take the initiative with a realistic proposal of your own. In this instance, I thought this tactic might be worth considering as an option. My friend considered his alternatives and decided that he'd go back to the vendor with a response a little more comprehensive than 'no'. He proposed that unless the original verbal acceptance was followed up with solicitors' missives within two working days (making the acceptance legally binding), then that offer would be withdrawn and replaced with one £2,000 less than the original (accepted) amount. Making it clear that his intention was to make good on the original deal, and equally clear that kite flying for late concessions would only lead to equal and opposite costs.

On this occasion, the desired result was achieved with the verbally accepted original offer being formalised, and no additional late demands. Indeed, it was very much contributed to by my friend's thorough preparation, which gave him the opportunity to explore a wider range of options than simply hoisting his kite to see whether it'd fly...

Four rooms – Be careful of how far you drive price; you get what you pay for...

Alan Smith

(Published 12th December 2019)

(Based on a true-ish story)

Imagine the scene.

You decide to get your whole house repainted.

You invite four local firms to come to your home and give you a quote. After they have looked around, you sit each of them in a separate room and ask them for their best price.

Each of them has the same brief and needs to cover materials as well as labour. They all have two weeks to complete the job.

You ask them to write down their price, and you go to each room to collect their submission.

Having done so, you choose the lowest price, and then go into each room and ask each firm to match a price 10% below that number. If they can't, you thank them and ask them to leave.

Two of the firms tell you 'no'. One of them in a very fruity way (shame really, because one of the losers had worked on a neighbour's house and had done a great job, cleaning up each night, and coming back to touch up a scratch for free that was caused when their son moved his pool table into the hall).

Two are left.

Each say they can hit the price.

You say to the remaining two, now you need to give me a better price, sharpen your pencil, and give me another offer.

One asks will that win the business. You honestly say 'maybe' and walk out.

Both come up with a price. One sticks at the 10% reduction. The other gives you another 5% off that price.

You award the business to the lowest price.

During the work, the firm that you selected suggests that the materials you requested in the quote would not be viable in the bathrooms and kitchen. They offer to include the new paint at a higher price, along with new labour rates to cover the complexity and number of coats needed to apply.

They then tell you on the Friday night that they had not quoted for clearing up at the weekend. So, they would leave all the stuff out, unless of course you paid overtime.

You reluctantly agree; you don't fancy stepping around paint tins all weekend, or having to redo the kitchen next year.

Four weeks after they have finished, you notice that the lounge is already looking shabby. You call the decorator. They say the paper you selected needed to be lined, which they didn't do in order to hit the price and deadline you imposed. They offer to get one of their competitors to give you a call to get it redone. Ironically, it was one of the firms that walked out after the first round of price pressure in the four rooms.

Is there a moral to this tale?

There are many, to be honest. The first is to be careful what you wish for. If you are genuinely using price to select who you work with, be careful that you do not destroy any potential relationship or find yourself working with people who do whatever they can to get you back and make money in other creative ways. Purely transactional relationships are pretty rare really.

If you are tempted to enter these 'auction' style scenarios, make sure you do not give everything away in the first, second or maybe third round. Perhaps the other side will still want another bite at the cherry.

Moreover, recognise that maybe you should walk away early to fight another day. You will not be able to win every opportunity that comes your way. Unless you have a strategic reason for the volume, profit and margin should be the barometer. Top line for vanity, profit for sanity.

By the way, none of the above is a negotiation. It is a series of positional plays.

Negotiation requires us to create value, not just argue over who takes it all.

The best negotiations leave all parties prepared to put the deal into practice. Otherwise, one of you might take a pasting.

Internet shopping – Not as much as you could wish for? – The advantages of bargaining face to face...

David Bannister

(Published 23rd July 2015)

I was reading my newspaper recently and came across an article written by a journalist who was celebrating the demise of, as she called it, the 'shiny suited car salesman' whose sexist attitudes have apparently in the past been responsible for women being urged to do things like 'discuss their purchases with the man of the house' before making a decision.[28] This article set out, to me, some quite eye-opening statistics for the UK market in new and 'pre-owned' (it's what they call second-hand here) cars. The internet has liberated people to change their purchasing habits when they buy a car. In the days before the internet dominated our buying approach, the average Briton buying a car made five visits to a dealership before making a purchase. Now, most of us do our research online. You can choose your new car, sort out the finance for it and arrange the part exchange of your old car, and even arrange delivery without setting eyes on a single shiny suit. Footfall in car dealerships in the UK has apparently fallen by over 60% in the last 10 years. What a revolution! It is said that the second largest purchase we all make after a house is a car and we are moving to doing that without any human interaction – amazing! Or is it? When I bought my current car, I did what we teach in Scotwork – I enriched the deal by talking one to one with the dealer and getting a few extras to make the purchase just that bit sweeter and more personal. For Jane, my wife, the important extra was a fluffy teddy bear dressed in a T-shirt bearing the manufacturer's logo, which she introduced as 'just one more thing' as my pen hovered over the contract papers!

Have you ever tried to negotiate with your laptop? Let me tell you it doesn't work. I wonder if this move to internet buying is really something that works to the advantage of the

---

[28] www.telegraph.co.uk/motoring/11751502/The-death-of-the-slimy-sexist-car-salesmen.html

sellers much of the time. Their headline on the website may be price, but what about all of the other things we value when we buy that shiny lump of metal to sit on the driveway and make a statement to our neighbours? Is it important to have it picked up and dropped off when it has its annual service? Will they throw in a fluffy teddy?

Are we prospective car buyers being put in a place that serves the dealers' aims and reduces our negotiating scope? I really don't know, but I suggest that the next time you want some new wheels, you should do your research by all means, but take the time to have a meeting with the man in the shiny suit and see how much he wants your business and if he has got your equivalent of a fluffy teddy bear to ensure that you get it from him.

Who do you think you are? – Progressive bargaining for a better deal...

Stephen White

(Published 7th June 2018)

Some years ago, I inherited a scruffy, handwritten family tree from an elderly uncle, listing my father's forebears. Intrigued and interested, I did some research and expanded it, including my mother's family, and then my wife's family. When the technology became available, I used a web-based programme to put it online and make it accessible to others. As a result, distant relatives I didn't know existed contacted me and the tree grew even taller and wider. Genealogy had turned into one of my hobbies.

In this endeavour research is fundamental. Access to census and church records, immigration papers, newspaper archives and suchlike is available on the web, but the providers are all subscription-based services and their charges are substantial.

So, I was pleasantly surprised to get an email yesterday from *My Heritage*, one of the providers whom I had used some years ago, offering me a year's access to all their research resources at half price. I clicked through the email to the website, checked out the deal and decided to go for it. I clicked to accept and started to fill in my details.

I got as far as my first name when the phone rang. 'Hello, is that Stephen?' Yes. 'This is Roy from *My Heritage*. I know you used to be a subscriber and I have seen some recent activity from you on our website. I am calling to offer you an even better deal than the one you are considering now.'

Freaky coincidence? No, I don't believe in that. Malware on my computer which is spying on me? No, I have all the necessary protection. This was marketing automation – technology enabling the website to hit me with a sales pitch as soon as activity from my IP address suggested I might be interested in buying.

My first reaction was indignation – who the hell did they think they were invading my privacy? Milliseconds later this was replaced by curiosity. What was the better deal?

Roy offered me a couple of extra freebies, which were high priced but of little value to me, and a £15 gift voucher. I politely declined and asked instead for the half price deal to be extended for a second year. I was put on hold. He came back and offered me a small discount for the second year. I declined again and said I'd probably just go for the one-year deal. I was put on hold again. He came back with a more substantial discount for the second year. I asked if I would get a £15 gift voucher for each year. He said he would have to call me back. He did and agreed. The deal was done. Both parties were satisfied – Roy earned his commission and I get to enjoy my hobby at a discount.

There is no doubt that I was more susceptible to a sales pitch at the point that Roy made the call. That is the point of the automation technology. But susceptibility is not the same as surrender. There is often a better deal – if you look for it.

Sack Black Friday – Deals are often not as good as they seem; act with caution...

Alan Smith

(Published 28th November 2019)

If you think Black Friday offers good deals, you may be right. But good deals for who is a very different question.

Black Friday is a colloquial name for the Friday following Thanksgiving; which in turn is celebrated in the US on the fourth Thursday of November. The day after Thanksgiving has been regarded as the beginning of America's Christmas shopping bonanza since 1952, and subsequently exported globally, although the term 'Black Friday' did not become widely used until more recent times.

Why Black?

Well, it describes the traffic, bad vibes and overall hysteria of punters looking for good deals. Fighting over them in the store aisles and spending in a wild, panic-driven frenzy by our ancient hunting instincts (or so it appears). Billions are spent, making it one of the busiest shopping weekends of the year.

Retailers (on and offline) have got in on the act by promoting deals and encouraging us to part with our hard-earned cash, on amazing deals on anything our hearts desire (or advertising convinces us we need). I'm not sure my dog actually does need a Prada dog carrier for £1,500, thank you.

But are these 'deals' any good?

Well, they are not according to *Which?*. At least not for the consumer.

Which? suggests that only 1 in 20 of the Black Friday deals represent any kind of financial saving. They found that 95% of the Black Friday deal items they investigated – which included popular tech, home and personal care products – were available for the same price or cheaper in the six months after.

A couple of tips they suggest:

- Shop around; same price in multiple stores? Look out;
- Be aware of RRP comparisons. Who sells at RRP?;
- Look for notes 'explaining' offers. Me thinks thou does protest too much.

For the 5% that do work to make a deal a good deal, make sure you want what it is you are buying. Sounds obvious but I remember buying a pair of salmon pink chinos in the sale (great price) and throwing them away six months later, unworn (should have given them to my mate Nick Ford, he likes salmon pink chinos, but he's much taller than me).

Don't get excited by deals. Breathe first. Wander around then think what would life be like if you didn't own it. The same? Walk away.

Now, unless you just won millions on the lottery, think: can I afford this? Getting into debt on a deal makes it a bad deal. Any savings wiped out by the credit card bill that hits the mat.

Also, think about who is this a good deal for? Probably the retailer who has been sitting on the stock for months and sees the chance to shift some gear (salmon pink chinos for example).

I am always wary of people who offer me great deals. I think they have probably set up their pricing, terms and value proposition in a way to make me think I've won, when they expected the very deal on the table after the discussion in the first place.

Want to negotiate? Start there; after the first dance there is usually another.

Do you want a cake or just a slice of cake? – Good negotiators think value, NOT price...

David Bannister

(Published 2ⁿᵈ September 2021)

Some years ago, when I was early in my independent consulting career, I won a substantial piece of work with a prestigious international client in manufacturing. My associates and I were to produce a set of nine training modules to help their leadership development group to work with the business's technical development teams to become better at virtual working in all its aspects. This company had global development teams working collaboratively and sharing expertise across many different countries; this was facilitated through virtual meetings held in specially equipped facilities in their offices long before the word Zoom had got further than the Batman comics!

At my first meeting with my sponsor, all went well: plans were approved, timetables agreed and the content and general emphasis of the work confirmed. But right at the end of a half-day meeting, my sponsor unexpectedly said, 'The only problem is your price, the budget approved can only be £X' (a figure of about 80% of what was in my detailed and, I thought, agreed proposal). I threw my stunned brain into gear and it told me that this was a ploy – the previous three and a half hours of detailed discussion would never have taken place with this major barrier unresolved. I suspect that he had tried this before and the supplier, terrified of losing the work at the last minute, had caved in. Trying hard to look cool and unruffled (I didn't feel it), I said something along the lines of, 'What a shame. Have you considered which two of the modules you will not be needing us to write for you?'. My sponsor said, with a poker face he must have practised before, 'Leave it with me, I will see what we can do.' A couple of days later, he sent me a short email asking me to proceed with all nine modules at the proposed price. We completed the project and were paid for them as proposed.

I was reminded of this recently when my wife, who is an excellent and skilled baker, retired from her job and decided that she would commercially bake 'occasion' cakes, which she had previously limited, for reasons of time, to doing only for family members. Inevitably, she had to consider how much she would charge for these creations and she consulted friends in her specialist bakers' internet forum and also me. These cakes require a lot of time and expertise and are inevitably priced accordingly. Much debate centres around whether customers would pay a price that reflected the many hours the bakers spend on the cakes and the fact that the customers would probably have no clue about how long it takes to make a cake that looks like their daughter's much-loved pony or reflects their son's obsession with JCBs (I recognise this is sexist, but trust me, it has never happened the other way round!). The view they all came to (with some contribution from yours truly) was that if you want a cake that looks exactly like a bottle of champagne, and from which you can actually pour champagne, this will be the price. If that is too much money, you (the customer) can choose a different, cheaper cake, a smaller bottle cake, a bottle cake that is solid and doesn't pour champagne, or you can go to Tesco and buy an off-the-shelf mass-produced cake that looks like everyone else's birthday cake. If you want the best, it will not be cheap. It was an interesting and largely academic debate – these bakers are very skilled and their talents are in short supply. Nevertheless, it was an important principle to establish and they now need to hold the circle. There is no merit in being the baker who says a price and then backs down and cuts it (forgive the pun).

As a lawyer friend of mine once said to me, 'I don't discount, discounts are forever, they raise expectations for next time and never get smaller.'

After this discussion, one of the forums posted this picture to the members.

I love it because it says, I am really good at what I do but if you won't pay me properly for what I am good at, you will not get the thing I am good at – you will get what you pay for and as I will not compromise my standards you probably won't get me to do your baking/consulting/painting/car repair or whatever.

Here are some of the cakes made:

THE 8-STEPS

CHAPTER 7

CLOSE TO GETTING THE DEAL OVER THE LINE

You've done all the hard work and both parties have almost reached a point where a deal can be struck. At or towards the end of the negotiation there is often an opportunity to draw out issues that have not been finalised, which can provide an opportunity for 'trial closing'. For example, if the other party brings hidden or unresolved issues to the table, you ask the question, 'Are you saying that if I agree to those items, you will be satisfied with the whole deal?'.

Similarly, if there is a question about a minor aspect of your proposal, rather than saying 'yes' or 'no', your answer is that if the other party agrees to the overall proposal you are prepared to concede on these (specific and minor) points.

There can be a tendency here to get greedy; you don't want to snatch a dispute from the jaws of a compromise by being too competitive, so resist the impulse to do so.

Muck shift – Just when is a deal not a deal...?

Robin Copland

(Published 14ᵗʰ May 2015)

I heard this story from a friend of mine; there are some lessons to be learned!

So, my pal is a developer and is building some houses on what was essentially a square site. Two sides of the square can be accessed from the road in a neighbouring housing estate and the other two are beside a field owned by another developer. There is a huge pile of muck to shift before the actual building project; this phase is known in the trade (and not unreasonably) as a 'muck shift'! There were to be 80 to 100 lorries coming in and out each day for six weeks, and it was considered more convenient to access the site over the field, so an approach was made to the developer to discuss the terms under which he would allow access. This is a fairly standard arrangement, and the deal typically is that the field would be returned to the owner in its original condition. The developer makes a bit of money, where otherwise he wouldn't, homeowners in the adjoining estate are less inconvenienced, and the builder does not need to spend money cleaning the streets and getting them back to a usable state at the end of the project. Win-win.

After a bit of haggling (it could never have been described as a negotiation), where my pal made an initial offer of

£19.5k, a figure of £26.5k was agreed. Hands were shaken and a contract was forwarded to the other developer, who returned it unsigned, saying that a 'gentlemen's agreement' had been reached. A week before the lorries were due to roll, he got back in touch asking for more money. So much for the 'gentlemen's agreement'! The builders, resourceful chaps that they are, had another look at the problem and came up with a perfectly safe, do-able alternative access plan that, though not perfect from the homeowners' perspective, would involve access to the site without using the developer's field at all.

My pal went back to the owner of the field. He thanked him for helping to identify a cheaper solution but politely declined to pay more than the £26.5k that had been agreed as part of the original 'gentlemen's agreement'. In fact, armed with his builder's alternative solution, my pal went further. 'Given that you reneged on the original agreement of £26.5k, we now consider that deal as off the table. We are reverting to our original offer of £19.5k,' and, he added, 'that is our final position.'

The developer held out, unaware that there was an alternative solution. My pal implemented the alternative and the developer missed out on £26.5k.

Moral of the tale?

Be careful with whom you shake hands. It is a sad fact of life perhaps, but deals are better made in writing and contractually – even, it seems, in Scotland, whose legal system has long allowed for such a contract.

Be aware of your negotiating limit.

Don't get greedy.

And if someone fights fire with fire and comes out with guns blazing, it might be desperation – or they might just know something you don't...

Members of the jury!! – The power of a powerful, unifying final statement (of intent)

Alan Smith

(Published 10ᵗʰ May 2018)

If any of you have been in jury service, I'm sure you'll agree. It's fascinating.

Can't tell you anything about the deliberation, it's against the law. Could tell you about the verdict, but not going to, not relevant to my story (oh, go on then, guilty!)

The thing that I really enjoyed watching was the to-and-fro between the various advocates in the court, and indeed the judge. I do not want to be flippant about this in any way, as in the end, the cases dealt with some pretty traumatic events in people's lives, but to a keen observer of behaviour and our reactions to it, what a microcosm to behold.

As a commercial negotiator, I saw a couple of key observations.

The first was that despite the obvious skill of the barristers in telling wonderfully persuasive stories and weaving compelling narratives, neither of them particularly saved the day for either side. In fact, and to be honest, after a while I kind of switched off. Well, they would say that, wouldn't they? A bit like a salesman blathering on about a product you were going to buy anyway (or not).

The art of getting others to see things how you see them is brilliant when it works. But pretty blooming dull when it doesn't. No one likes being preached to. Well, maybe they do but only in church.

The second was the absolute power of the final summary from the judge.

This summary was a brief overview of all major arguments in the case, delivered in a compelling and dispassionate way. All the main facts and arguments were presented in a manner that removed all the confusing but inevitable emotion and pulled together the threads that both sides presented. It was remarkably powerful.

A final summary in a negotiation is often overlooked, as everyone leans back in awe of the deal they have just struck. Try to ensure this does not happen. Get everyone on the same page and identify any misunderstandings. Lots of deals fall apart or need to be revisited due to this one simple oversight.

The other thing a summary should not be is biased. If you want the summary to be valid, make sure it is a genuine summary of both sides. Totally partial summaries only focused on what you want to believe or happen destroy any vestiges of trust and are likely to destroy a relationship or deal rather than create one.

It ain't over... – Keeping dealing to the very end...

Alan Smith

(Published 14ᵗʰ December 2017)

The maxim 'it ain't over till it's over' is a maxim because it's true.

Fans of Queens Park Rangers (QPR) were lambasted by their manager for leaving before the end in a match against local rivals, Brentford.

At 2–0 down and into injury time, many of the QPR fans decided to leave their home stadium, Loftus Road, and missed what makes sport remarkable – two late goals from QPR to clutch a draw from the jaws of defeat from their local rivals.

Ian Holloway, the then QPR manager said, 'I was disappointed with our fans, I'd like to say. You should have stayed. You might have missed your last bus, but you missed a treat. For me, it feels like a win, for them it probably feels like a defeat.'

The point is quite clear – stay with it until the end or you very much may miss something.

Negotiators should be absolutely clear about this too. Often there is significant value lost, or indeed gained, in the final stages of the negotiation. When one or other sides recognise that the negotiation is nearly done, the trained negotiator looks to improve or sweeten the deal. So much effort has gone into securing a negotiating agreement that it can be difficult to say 'no' to a last request, which occasionally turns into the penultimate request rather than the last one after all.

Keep your wits about you and make sure you are able to use last, small requests as an opportunity to trade for something that you would like too, or at least try to use it as an opportunity to trade for the negotiation to close.

Of course, it is very much in your interests to keep asking for value until the other side says enough. You are commercially responsible for yourself, not them – but don't get greedy!

Another sporting icon, Eddie Jones, ex-manager of the England rugby team, has found a motivational way of rebranding his substitutes as 'finishers', who come on in the last quarter of a match to finish the game plan and blast away the opposition. To great impact, wins against Australia and Samoa were sealed conclusively in the last five minutes.

While I would not necessarily advocate finishers in negotiation, it is certainly worth spending a small amount of time before the final agreement with your initial negotiating objectives and a well-prepared value building list to try to bridge any gaps in your plan.

Certainly, before you get into any singing, fat person or otherwise.

Getting into hot water – When faced with two sources of legitimate information, don't sit on the fence, make a call...

Stephen White

(Published 17th September 2020)

We had a kitchen tap problem. No hot water. We don't have a regular plumber, but coincidentally that same day we had received a tradesmen's flyer, so we went with one of the plumbers listed.

He turned up on time, he was a very nice man and he seemed to know what he was talking about. He assessed the problem, diagnosed elderly pipework, did some more tests, re-diagnosed elderly pipework plus a faulty tap and told us what we needed to replace it with – a new tap capable of handling low water pressure because of the pipework.

There and then we found a tap on Amazon – he checked the specification and said it was fine. We'd call back when the tap was delivered. Two days later it arrived. We called him and made an appointment for later that week. The following day a second tap arrived – I had inadvertently ordered twice. We returned one to Amazon.

The plumber arrived. He looked at the tap and declared it unfit for purpose. The hose to the tap, which attaches to the pipework, was too narrow for low water pressure. We would need to select again. He'd come back when we had a suitable tap. We returned the second tap to Amazon, feeling foolish. Without hot water, washing up was an increasingly tiresome process.

We found online a tap warehouse, which happened to be about four miles from our home. We selected a tap that was specifically designed for low-pressure systems, then called the warehouse and asked if we could come to check it out and take it home. They were very nice but no, the showroom was closed because of Covid. Could they assure me the tap was suitable for low water pressure? Yes, it was, and if the tap was wrong, they would refund. And delivery would be £10. I asked if I could avoid the £10 charge, being so close to the warehouse. Perhaps someone could just drop it round on their way home? No, but they immediately offered me a £12 discount on the price of the tap, then added back the £10 for delivery. I was now £2 better off.

The tap arrived. The plumber arrived. Alas, this tap was also unfit for purpose, for the same reason. The hoses were too narrow.

At which point I had to work out who was the most dysfunctional – the tap warehouse, the plumber, or me? Despite my complete ignorance of plumbing and taps I reckoned it wasn't me, and of the other two choices, I decided on instinct to trust the warehouse. So I told the plumber to fit the tap regardless of his view, and that I would take responsibility if it didn't work.

It worked fine. The plumber was baffled. It wasn't designed to work, it shouldn't have worked, but he could see with his own eyes that it obviously did work. There must be a gizmo inside the tap he didn't know about which made it work.

Whatever. We now had hot water in the kitchen sink.

Moral of the story? In negotiations, if you are dealing with two sources of information both of which seem legitimate, it is better to make a decision and go with your instinct rather than be stuck with indecision. Sometimes you'll get it right, sometimes not, but at least making a decision keeps the momentum flowing.

Like the tap.

How do you measure success? – Focus on your objectives, not screwing the other party...

Alan Smith

(Published 31st May 2018)

What a great question. And one I was asked recently by a client who was interested in figuring out a metric by which they could measure deals to figure out if they were good or not.

I am sure in the past we have all sat back as the ink begins to dry on the contract, and wondered if the deal was a good one, could we have pushed a bit harder, conceded a little less, got a bit more volume or a longer deal; did we really need to piss off the other side quite so much, or could we have pissed them off a bit more without damaging the long term?

Truth is we will never really know, except in cases as when I once switched sides from client to agency and realised how valuable my account had been to the other side.

Having spent the last 10 years in the sphere of negotiation it seems to me that there are three core metrics we need to consider: outcomes, efficiency and relationship.

Possibly the most consistent guide to performance is the time and inventiveness you put into your preparation for an upcoming negotiation. What you have done, or indeed not done, will become blatantly obvious once the process starts. If we have spent time identifying what a good deal looks like in preparation and have thought creatively and flexibly as to how it could be attained, your outcomes will be better (and if not, you will not have wasted too much time in chasing something that you simply should not be chasing anyway). 'Have I achieved my objectives?' is the priority measurement.

Have I been efficient in managing the negotiation process? Despite all the crystal-ball-gazing in the past telling us that mechanisation will create so much efficiency that we will have time aplenty on our hands, the truth, for now, is that time is a much scarcer commodity than ever. Not just at work either.

Managing the negotiation process effectively means that we need to recognise the process in the first place (what

Scotwork call the 8-Steps) and use the appropriate skill at the appropriate time to navigate that process with proficiency. Have I used time appropriately or have I been rudderless, drifting without clarity and direction?

I recently received a call from a client who was delighted that since attending our training sessions not only had he managed to build more value into the deals he and his team had been doing, but he had also managed to do this while building relationships.

Driving a hard deal may create a short-term win, but in the long term may create problems. All sides need to see some skin in the game if the objective is to find ways of creating value via the negotiation process.

So, did I get the best deal available; did I drive the other side to their walk-away point?

Of course, in reality, you may never know, but if I've achieved my objectives efficiently, while maintaining a good relationship, I think I've done alright.

THE 8-STEPS

CHAPTER 8

AGREE AND DOCUMENT WHAT HAS BEEN AGREED

It is important to agree what has been agreed, whereby you ensure there are no ambiguities, the actions for implementation are agreed, the agreement is confirmed and documented and they are willing to put it in place. Many deals turn sour as insufficient attention has been paid to how the deal will be implemented.

Precision blindness – The devil's in the detail; ignore it at your peril...

Horace McDonald

(Published 19th May 2022)

Some years ago, I met a mergers and acquisitions specialist who worked for a multinational PLC. Their job was to assess acquisition targets, weigh them up, assess strategic fit and make recommendations on the suitability of a purchase. It seems very interesting, challenging and demanding work requiring high levels of analysis and some degree of intuition. Businesses doing deals on this scale pay vast amounts of money to professional advisers as the nature of these deals is often very complex, and negotiations drawn out and often finalised in a rush to satisfy the deadlines of the market.

He told me a story about a recent acquisition, where on completion of the deal, with everything signed and sealed, the acquired company realised that a major error in the drafting could result in their company losing significant sums of money. It resulted in the CEO of that company calling the acquiring company's CEO to have the clause changed. At this point the acquiring company's CEO had two choices: they could re-open the whole deal with a view to extracting value as compensation for changing the clause or they could pick one item that added value to them as compensation. However, the problem was so vast to the other party that this second option was rendered untenable. The view taken was that each party is paid to look after their own interests and they had both invested huge sums in advisers. As the company was being acquired outright and the deal was signed, they did not see any advantage being gained from changing the deal. An example writ large (maybe not large enough) of how negotiation is only one way of resolving conflict and will always result in you having to give something away. In this instance, the acquiring CEO decided to resolve the conflict without having to negotiate.

A similar and more whimsical example of the same problem beset Giuseppe Reina, a German professional footballer, who in 1996 signed for DSC Arminia Bielefeld in the Bundesliga. He inserted a clause into his contract requiring the club to build him a house for every year he was under contract with the club (a total of three years). However, Reina became a victim of unclear drafting when the club built him a house made out of LEGO for each year he was under contract, as he had not stipulated the size of the house.

One of the challenges in negotiation is that much time is spent in what we call the **Argue** Step, where each party seeks to make their position clear and, more importantly, to understand the interests of the other party.[29] Often too much time is spent articulating their own position and the above suggests that more time spent focusing on the details of the deal can make a huge difference.

Climate of change – Assume nothing until the money's in the bank...

Stephen White

(Published 8th June 2017)

The *London Evening Standard* reported some time ago, and if you had seen it would have given you a quiet moment of

---

[29] www.scotwork.co.uk/solutions/ans/

schadenfreude, that Cherie Blair, the eminent barrister, was gazumped. The story went that she offered £2.75m for a house in Marylebone and her offer was accepted, until the twice ex-wife of Elon Musk, actress Talulah Riley, bid £3m and stole it from under her nose.

Picture the scene. For the seller the offer of an extra quarter of a million is irresistible, and the celebrity down-trading from the wife of a past Prime Minister to the star of two St Trinian's films is hardly slumming it. Blair no doubt was relaxed in the expectation that no one would mess around with a high-profile lawyer and will have been spitting feathers when she was outbid after she thought the deal was done. But, although it may be unethical and immoral, there is nothing illegal in England about gazumping and her only remedy would have been to bid even higher.

Fast forward to another high-profile piece of gazumping. When, early in his presidential career, Donald Trump pulled out of the Paris Accord on climate change, he and his spokes-people made it clear that he was not heading for the hills, he simply wanted to renegotiate a deal which was 'fairer for the US', notwithstanding that the deal was already done and that the Accord in its present form had been ratified by 148 of the 195 countries who signed it.

Trump wanted a better deal, and his tactic of reneging on the agreement (like the house seller did) poses all sorts of problems for his fellow country heads. They might complain about his lack of ethics and morals, they might write open letters to his administration appealing to his better side (does he have one?), but they have no legal remedy and the climate change talks reopened as a result.

Negotiating deals relies on trust; that the parties to the deal will stick to their word and perform on their agreements. In our increasingly uncertain world, the propensity to play dirty has eroded the value of trust to the point that negotiators need to realise that the deals they do are potentially all at risk. Negotiators used to say that it wasn't a deal until the ink was dry on the order form. Nowadays, it isn't a deal until the goods have been delivered and the money is in the bank.

So, what suggestions are there for a potential gazumpee? As usual in our Uncertainty Series, here is one piece of advice on strategy, tactics and skill.

- **Strategy**: Keep the timeline as short as possible. The longer the opportunity to unpick a deal, the more likely it is to happen. If Blair could have completed the deal in a few days maybe neither the seller nor Riley would have had the opportunity to disrupt it. The Paris Accord was not scheduled to start for another four years. Not a wise move – elements of it should have kicked in straight away.

- **Tactics**: Use the lock-in tactic to minimise the risk. In house purchases, both seller and purchaser commit a small percentage of the price, typically 2-3%, to a contract which commits both parties to go through with the deal except in certain specific exceptional situations. If the contract is broken by either party outwith these exceptions, then the contracted percentage is forfeited. All signatories to the Paris Accord could have been locked in in the same way.

- **Skill:** Do some homework before you make an offer. Not about the property but about the seller. Have they been trying hard to sell? Is the sale a distress situation (they need the money badly)? Does the estate agent speak well of them? Do you have any links – friends of friends – who might be dropped into a conversation? Manufacturing a closer relationship than is really true might make the potential gazumper more reserved about doing it to you.

Getting it done!! – Make sure that everyone in the deal understands their responsibilities in its implementation...

Alan Smith

(Published 10ᵗʰ October 2019)

It is quite easy to see the problem of negotiators being involved in the deal, but not in the act of putting the deal into practice.

The sales team, who are committed to delivering on their targets, may not be that concerned about what happens at the implementation stage, or, worse, may leave it to others to pick up the pieces when they over-promise or throw everything in to get the signature on the paper.

Or the buyers in 'professional' procurement teams who drive down the price so aggressively that the work cannot possibly be done to the required quality, setting up complaints and relationship challenges down the line.

Compliance as part of the process surely must play its part.

When my youngest daughter started her second year at university, she experienced the very same problems of fulfilment with her four housemates.

Prior to going back, she had spent quite a lot of time over the summer in agreeing on the tasks that would need to be shared between the five of them (all female medical students, not that that has anything to do with the story). How they would deal with cleaning shared spaces, who would put out the bins, how they would pay for shared services and products (like toilet paper). I suspect that providing your own toilet cleaning and loo roll is one of the big growing up experiences in life. Like realising Father Christmas is not real and the tooth fairy is usually a parent looking for spare coins before creeping into your bedroom, it's a sad and heartbreaking insight.

Anyway, they all agreed to a cleaning rota, deposited their hard-earned (not by them I'd hasten to add) coins in the bog bank tin and proceeded to the bar to enjoy student life.

Early in the term she called home and proceeded to rant about how the others were not living up to the agreed deal. Dirty dishes everywhere. Bin overflowing. Toilets encrusted (apologies to those of you with delicate constitutions) with effluent from both ends.

One of the girls said she didn't think they needed a toilet brush as they would not be cleaning the toilets anyway!! For four years!!!

While I giggled internally to myself (growing up is a long and intricate process), it did make me realise that how a deal works in practice is not limited to the world of work.

How do we resolve this?

Well, the first thing is to call it out. The number of times I have heard from my clients, who have put well-structured deals in place, that the other side has not delivered the volumes they promised, or the skilled staff they had agreed, and have just carried on with the deal is remarkable. Make the other side at least aware of where they have overstepped the mark from the get-go.

Really important before you agree any deal is to spend time on figuring out implementation and the implications of things changing, going wrong or simply not being delivered.

Think about what problems may come up. Critically communicate a consistent and well-structured message about the deal, its terms and the spirit it has been entered into.

And don't be afraid to go back to the negotiating table if one side is not living up to the agreed deal. Compliance to a non-performing deal is not for the sake of the relationship, it is a destruction of it.

I offered to help my daughter with her challenge. She refused. Another part of growing up, I guess. And one I am in big favour of.

EPILOGUE

It's a dog's life – All 8-Steps in one...

Introduction

I recently got chatting with Laura, a participant on a Scotwork course, about our mutual love of dogs. Both being the new families of relatively young dogs, we shared the ups and downs of dog ownership. Photos were exchanged and eyes were rolled in mutual understanding of the midnight trips to the garden, but all in all it was clear that we were both besotted with our canine chums.

The gorgeous girl in the photo here is Lexi and shortly after the course her Mum, Laura, sent me a delightful message sharing how she had used her new skills with her worthy four-legged opponent.

Here is Laura and Lexi's story in the former's own words.

I thought one of my recent uses of my new negotiation skills might amuse you 😊:

We recently came home with a new toy, her now favourite toy. However, we soon faced an issue and my new skills were put to the test – Lexi wanted to take the toy on her walk but I didn't want it to go outside and get dirty. We were at an impasse and I thought this was a good opportunity to use my negotiation tactics with my little fur ball.

I made a mental list of what I had to trade with her, with a wish list and concession list at the ready.

Argue: 'Lexi will you drop your toy so that we can go for a walk?' She doesn't budge. I ask again, she proudly starts walking around with it in her mouth; she will not back down. We are stuck in a circular argument. However, she is showing clear signals that she really wants to go on the walk so there might be an in.

Propose: 'If you drop the toy, I will give you a treat.' She considers it but then walks away, it hasn't worked.

I go back to the drawing board, need a better package. I work on an improved offer but it is clear I can't move on the toy not going outside at this point so I need to find ways around it, something I can bargain.

New proposal: 'You drop the toy and I will give you a buffalo chew while I get ready.' This has piqued her interest; she drops the toy, this could conclude the deal but she isn't across the line. I look at my concession list, 'Okay *if* you drop the toy I *will* let you have a buffalo chew in the garden in the sun (her favourite)'. She is wagging her tail, I think we could close, but I quickly think of my wish list and throw in, 'But you give me extra cuddles when we come back in from the walk'... She thinks... she waggles, she jumps up and licks my chin, *we are agreed!*

There is a structure underpinning all negotiations which can be used skilfully to achieve success in all manner of situations. Of course, understanding the structure is one thing; using it successfully can often be quite another! The benefits of building skill around structure can yield huge rewards in all areas of our life. After all, negotiation is a life skill, not just a commercial skill... even when you're just trying to take your best friend for a walk!

Author biographies

John McMillan (Scotwork Founder)

I started negotiating when I ran the university student publications department and later in my job as a sales engineer. Nobody taught me what to do as there was no training available.

In 1975 when I set up Scotwork, intending to do something completely different, I recognised this was a need in the market that was not being addressed. Using my personal experience and some insights of others, I created our flagship course, now called Advancing Negotiating Skills.

The four things I enjoy the most are: crafting a deal where the value is greater than the sum of the parts; trading opinions where being correct pays off; meeting someone years later who says, "It was the best course I ever attended"; and finally walking away from the deal. This last is so much fun that I almost will the other side to give me a reason to walk. This conditions my thought process throughout the negotiation and removes any fear of the counterparty's sanction threats.

Alan Smith

I've spent the last 40 years of my commercial career dealing with 'misaligned objectives' between parties. The trouble is, most people think that the misalignment has been caused by an inability to persuade the other side(s) of the validity and quality of their position.

Since joining Scotwork as a negotiation consultant almost 17 years ago, the prism through which I view such differences has changed. Of course, if I recognise that I may be able to convince you to see things my way I'll stop there. But if I can find a different solution that recognises your needs and delivers them in a way that creates a better outcome for me, it is easier to come to an agreement that cements our relationship.

Stephen White

Trained as a lawyer, with experience in big-company sales and marketing, I realised early in my career that negotiating expertise did not come easily to most people. There were many books and theories but not much to help negotiators pragmatically in their working environment. Teaching the Scotwork course revealed to me that well-told stories about real negotiations resonated with our audiences more than anything else. This book contains some of those stories.

Romana Henry

My negotiating experience is steeped deeply in alcohol – scotch whisky, gin and vodka. The drinks world is a great industry to taste the various flavours of global negotiating in private label and branded products. I am also very active in sport. What have I learned? That like in any sport and as a keen sportsperson, no matter how long we've been playing the game, we must continue to learn more, practise and hone our skills in order to remain at the top.

Horace McDonald

Before joining Scotwork, I worked in sales, general management and leadership roles in FMCG and the music industry and encountered vastly different styles and approaches. The best thing about being an expert in negotiation is when someone asks me what I do for a living (you'd be surprised how many people don't know negotiation training is available) and their look of wonder when I give them my top three negotiation tips.

David Bannister

My long fascination with negotiating began when, as a young industrial relations officer, I sat in smoky rooms with union representatives learning the hard way about how tough it can be. Many years later, covering a career that has taken me all over the world and, as a consultant, into many different businesses, I know that when you have negotiating competence at your disposal, you will use these skills to good effect every day.

Robin Copeland

Robin has enjoyed his 33 years with Scotwork as both a consultant and director. He still helps out occasionally, but only at moments of extreme stress in the business! He ran courses in most sectors including retail, FMCG and energy. As well as running training events for Scotwork, he advised clients like the Financial Times, Scottish Hydro, Reckitt

Benckiser and News International on some of their trickier negotiations!

His interests include curling (past Scottish Champion), golf (definitely not past Scottish Champion!), photography, and Scottish transport history.

Tom Feinson

Born a twin I was introduced to conflict at an early age, causing rather than resolving. It wasn't until many years later that I became involved and fascinated by resolving conflict, you know what they say "To catch a thief…"

My time in negotiation has taken me across continents, included corporate giants as well as disruptor start-ups and straddled both not for profit and commercial sectors. It has always struck me that despite a myriad of contexts, cultures and styles negotiating behaviour is remarkably consistent. The stories in this book reveal the underlying structure to all negotiations and provide simple practical advice on effectively manging the negotiation process.

To give yourself an edge, understand what people are doing not just what they are saying.

Annabel Shorter

When the lure of a Vauxhall Cavalier proved too powerful, I entered the world of sales. As I moved on the deals got bigger and more complex and the ability to negotiate effectively while building strong relationships became ever more important. I believe our skills and strategies are often a powerful amalgam of everything we have seen, good and bad, from bosses, peers, parents and possibly even reality TV! Examining, questioning and improving can never be a bad thing.

Ellis Croft

There's an old saying about how to a man with a hammer, every problem looks like a nail. And that's how I – and many people, to be fair – used to negotiate. I didn't carry an actual hammer, just in case you were worrying. But I lacked an ability to assess, and options from which to choose in terms of negotiating better deals. A toolkit, even. Learning about the variety that choices give you and making some new mistakes instead of the old ones is fun, a pleasure and a privilege to share through some of the sillier stories I've been part of over the years.

Ann McAleavy

The last 28 years of my career has been in a sales environment, and I still get excited about work. Negotiation skills:, who knew there was such a requirement? Over the past 4 years I've eaten, slept, and breathed my job. Every morning with my music playing I almost dance on the drive into the office, the satisfaction of your client saying you helped them is intoxicating. Whether you're born to run or just tiptoeing, keep negotiating. These stories will give you a great insight to this understated skill.